SOUTH AMERICA

DELICIOUS SPANISH RECIPES FROM SOUTH AMERICA

By
BookSumo Press
Copyright © by Saxonberg Associates
All rights reserved

Published by
BookSumo Press, a DBA of Saxonberg Associates
http://www.booksumo.com/

About the Author.

BookSumo Press is a publisher of unique, easy, and healthy cookbooks.

Our cookbooks span all topics and all subjects. If you want a deep dive into the possibilities of cooking with any type of ingredient. Then BookSumo Press is your go to place for robust yet simple and delicious cookbooks and recipes. Whether you are looking for great tasting pressure cooker recipes or authentic ethic and cultural food. BookSumo Press has a delicious and easy cookbook for you.

With simple ingredients, and even simpler step-by-step instructions BookSumo cookbooks get everyone in the kitchen chefing delicious meals.

BookSumo is an independent publisher of books operating in the beautiful Garden State (NJ) and our team of chefs and kitchen experts are here to teach, eat, and be merry!

INTRODUCTION

Welcome to *The Effortless Chef Series*! Thank you for taking the time to purchase this cookbook.

Come take a journey into the delights of easy cooking. The point of this cookbook and all BookSumo Press cookbooks is to exemplify the effortless nature of cooking simply.

In this book we focus on South American cooking. You will find that even though the recipes are simple, the taste of the dishes are quite amazing.

So will you take an adventure in simple cooking? If the answer is yes please consult the table of contents to find the dishes you are most interested in.

Once you are ready, jump right in and start cooking.

— BookSumo Press

TABLE OF CONTENTS

About the Author 2
Introduction 3
Table of Contents 4
Any Issues? Contact Us 9
Legal Notes 10
Common Abbreviations 11
Chapter 1: Easy South American Recipes 12
    Brazilian Street Plantains 12
    Chimichurri Lunch Box Pitas 14
    Homemade Piri Piri 16
    How to Make a Flank Steak 18
    How to Make Dulce de Leche 20
    Halibut Griller 22
    Manioc Parmesan Bites 24
    (Pao de Queijo) 24
    Chicken Cutlets Chimichurri 26
    Porto Alegre Salsa 29
    Chimichurri Chicago Steak House 31
    Rabanada 33
    (Alternative French Toast) 33
    Chimichurri Mediterranean 35

Brazilian Fruit Shots 37

Flank Steak del Barrio 39

Collard Green Skillet 41

Chimichurri Aioli Glazed Tilapia 43

South American Avocado Smoothie 45

Argentinian x Mexico Bake 47

Brigadeiro (Mini Chocolate Truffles) 49

Chipotle Parsley Halibut 51

Cod and Coconut Stew 53

Sonoma Black Bean Tacos 55

Sao Paulo Poundcake 58

Catfish Córdoba 60

Sweet and Salty Raisin Rice 62

Chimichurri Lettuce Appetizers 64

Classic Dry Beef Chuck and Coconut Stew 66

Chimichurri Tilapia Cookout 68

South American Seafood Soup 70

Sopa de Papas con Chimichurri 72

Rice Skillet with Orange and Pimento 74

South American Beef Kebabs 76

Brazilian Vegetarian Hot Pot (Ginger and Coconut Curry) 78

Italian Tomato Chimichurri 80

Black Bean Stew I 82

Cinnamon Cayenne Rib Eye Clásico 84

Steak with Chimichurri 86

Argentinian Oatmeal Fries 88
Fortaleza Stroganoff 90
Chimichurri Zucchini and Squash with Potatoes 92
Brazilian Sausage 94
Burgers Argentino 96
Spicy Pink Shrimp 98
Orzo Calabasas 100
Potato Salad Brazilian II 102
Ginger Honey Glazed Kebabs 104
Brasileiro Skirts 107
Chiang Mai x Houston Chimichurri 109
Ambrosia Pudding 111
Chimichurri Shrimp 113
Habanero Rice 115
Burgers Brasileiro 117
Feijoada II 120
(Full Black Bean Stew) 120
Country Sirloin Argentinian 122
Brasileiro Flank 124
Chimichurri Route-66 126
Lime Glazed Sirloin 128
Fish with Tropical Mango Chimichurri 130
Goya Recaito and Seafood Stew 132
American-Mesa Chimichurri 134
Brazilian Long Grain II 136

Chimichurri Havana 138

Garlicky Chicken with Mango Salsa 140

6-Ingredient Steak with Mock Chimichurri... 143

Brazilian Shrimp Skillet 145

Roasted Peppermint Roast.. 147

Latin Flavored Butter 149

Eliza's Chimichurri 151

Catalina's Comfort Cake.. 153

Buenos Aires Brisket 155

Summer Night Banana Coffee Smoothie 157

Picnic Chimichurri 159

Savory Pineapple Steaks 161

Manhattan Strip Steaks... 163

Brazilian Wild Rice 165

Red Pepper Rib-Eye with Balsamic Chimichurri.................................... 167

Latin Leeks with Sweet Vinaigrette 169

Brazilian Casserole (Shrimp, Corn, and Parmesan and Peppers) 171

Cumin Coriander Flank Steak 173

Brazilian Potatoes 175

Rosario Chimichurri 177

Thursday's Latin Lunch Box Salad 179

Lemon Lime Skirt Steak with Chimichurri... 181

Kielbasa Stew 184

Creamy Coconut Cassava and Shrimp 186

Chipotle Shrimps 188

Pumpkin Bonbons...190
THANKS FOR READING! JOIN THE CLUB AND KEEP ON COOKING WITH 6 MORE COOKBOOKS...192
Come On... 194
Let's Be Friends :)..194

ANY ISSUES? CONTACT US

If you find that something important to you is missing from this book please contact us at info@booksumo.com.

We will take your concerns into consideration when the 2nd edition of this book is published. And we will keep you updated!

— BookSumo Press

LEGAL NOTES

ALL RIGHTS RESERVED. NO PART OF THIS BOOK MAY BE REPRODUCED OR TRANSMITTED IN ANY FORM OR BY ANY MEANS. PHOTOCOPYING, POSTING ONLINE, AND / OR DIGITAL COPYING IS STRICTLY PROHIBITED UNLESS WRITTEN PERMISSION IS GRANTED BY THE BOOK'S PUBLISHING COMPANY. LIMITED USE OF THE BOOK'S TEXT IS PERMITTED FOR USE IN REVIEWS WRITTEN FOR THE PUBLIC.

Common Abbreviations

cup(s)	C.
tablespoon	tbsp
teaspoon	tsp
ounce	oz.
pound	lb

*All units used are standard American measurements

Chapter 1: Easy South American Recipes

Brazilian Street Plantains

Ingredients

- 4 very ripe plantains (black skin)
- cooking spray

Directions

- Before you do anything, preheat the oven to 450 F.
- Grease a baking sheet with a cooking spray. Discard the plantain peel and slice it into 1/2 diagonal pieces.
- Lay the plantain pieces on the baking sheet. Cook it for 14 to 16 while flipping it halfway through.
- Once the time is up, allow the plantains slices to cool down completely then serve them.
- Enjoy.

Servings Per Recipe: 4

Timing Information:

| Preparation | 5 mins |
| Total Time | 20 mins |

Nutritional Information:

Calories	218.3
Fat	0.6g
Cholesterol	0.0mg
Sodium	7.1mg
Carbohydrates	57.0g
Protein	2.3g

* Percent Daily Values are based on a 2,000 calorie diet.

Chimichurri Lunch Box Pitas

Ingredients

- 1/2 tsp ground coriander
- 1/2 tsp ground cumin
- 1/2 tsp salt
- 1/4 tsp pepper
- 12 oz. boneless beef sirloin, sliced and cut into strips
- 2 tbsp olive oil, divided
- 2 C. yellow onions, cut in thin lengthwise
- 24 inches pita bread rounds
- 1/2 C. chimichurri sauce

Sauce:

- 2 C. loosely packed flat leaf parsley, and tender stems
- 1/4 C. coarsely chopped onion
- 2 tbsp extra-virgin olive oil
- 1/4 C. red wine vinegar
- 1 tbsp oregano leaves
- 4 garlic cloves
- 1/2 tsp cayenne pepper
- 1 pinch sugar
- salt and pepper

Directions

- For the Chimichurri sauce: in a food processor, add all the ingredients and pulse until smooth. In a large bowl, mix together the cumin, coriander, salt and pepper. Add the sirloin strips and coat with the spice mixture slightly. In a large skillet, heat 1 tbsp of the oil over medium-high heat and cook the onions for about 6 minutes, stirring occasionally. In the same skillet, add the beef and remaining 1 tbsp of the oil and cook for about 3 minutes, stirring occasionally. Remove from the heat and keep the aside, covered.
- Meanwhile, place the pitas onto a microwave-safe plate and with a paper towel, cover them. Microwave on High for about 1 minute.
- Cut each pita in half to form 2 pockets.
- Fill each pocket with the beef mixture.
- Place about 1 tbsp of the chimichurri sauce over each pocket and serve.

South America

Servings Per Recipe: 4

Timing Information:

| Preparation | 30 mins |
| Total Time | 45 mins |

Nutritional Information:

Calories	440.5
Fat	18.1g
Cholesterol	51.0mg
Sodium	658.2mg
Carbohydrates	42.8g
Protein	26.0g

* Percent Daily Values are based on a 2,000 calorie diet.

Homemade Piri Piri

Ingredients

- 4 tbsps lemon juice
- 5 tbsps olive oil
- 1/4 C. vinegar
- 1 tbsp cayenne pepper
- 1 tbsp garlic, minced
- 1 tbsp paprika
- 1 tsp salt
- 1 tbsp chili flakes

Directions

- Get a medium mixing bowl. Combine in it all the ingredients.
- Use this sauce to coat you chicken with it before grilling or roasting it in the oven. Serve it warm.
- Enjoy.

Servings Per Recipe: 1

Timing Information:

| Preparation | 5 mins |
| Total Time | 1 hr 20 mins |

Nutritional Information:

Calories	692.0
Fat	70.6g
Cholesterol	0.0mg
Sodium	2468.4mg
Carbohydrates	17.6g
Protein	3.4g

* Percent Daily Values are based on a 2,000 calorie diet.

How to Make a Flank Steak

Ingredients

Sauce:

- 1/2 C. flat leaf parsley, packed
- 2 tbsp lemon juice
- 1/2 tsp crushed red pepper flakes
- 1/4 tsp kosher salt
- 1/4 tsp sugar
- 1/4 tsp cumin
- 1 large garlic clove
- 2 tbsp extra virgin olive oil
- 1 tbsp water

Meat:

- 2 lb. flank steaks, trimmed
- 3/4 tsp kosher salt
- 1/2 tsp black pepper, freshly ground
- 2 garlic cloves, minced
- cooking spray

Directions

- Set your grill for medium-high heat and lightly, grease the grill grate.
- For the chimichurri sauce: in a food processor, add the garlic, parsley, lemon juice, sugar, cumin, red pepper flakes and salt and pulse until minced finely.
- While the motor is running, slowly add the oil and 1 tbsp of water and pulse until well combined.
- Rub the steak with the garlic clove evenly and then, sprinkle with the salt and pepper generously.
- Place the steak onto the grill and cook, covered for about 6 minutes.
- Flip and cook, covered for about 4 minutes.
- Transfer the steak onto a cutting board and cover with a piece of foil for about 5 minutes.
- Cut the steak into thin slices diagonally across the grain.
- Serve the steak slices alongside the Chimichurri sauce.

Servings Per Recipe: 8

Timing Information:

Preparation	10 mins
Total Time	25 mins

Nutritional Information:

Calories	222.1
Fat	12.8g
Cholesterol	77.1mg
Sodium	354.5mg
Carbohydrates	1.1g
Protein	24.3g

* Percent Daily Values are based on a 2,000 calorie diet.

HOW TO MAKE DULCE DE LECHE

Ingredients

- 1 can sweetened condensed milk

Directions

- Use a sharp knife of a bottle opener to pierce the top of the milk can.
- Remove the paper from the can and discard it.
- Place a large saucepan over medium heat. Place in it the milk can and pour it in the saucepan enough water to cover 1 inch of the can.
- Wrap a small piece of oil on top of the can and let it cook for 4 h over low medium heat.
- Once the time is up, discard the foil and open the milk can. Serve your dulce de leche with some cut up fruits, crackers…
- Enjoy.

Servings Per Recipe: 1

Timing Information:

Preparation	2 mins
Total Time	4 hrs 2 mins

Nutritional Information:

Calories	171.6
Fat	4.6g
Cholesterol	18.1mg
Sodium	67.9mg
Carbohydrates	29.0g
Protein	4.2g

* Percent Daily Values are based on a 2,000 calorie diet.

HALIBUT GRILLER

Ingredients

- 1 1/2 tbsp cilantro, chopped
- 1 tbsp basil, chopped
- 1 tbsp shallot, finely chopped
- 1 1/2 tbsp olive oil
- 1 1/2 tbsp lemon juice
- 1/2 tsp salt, divided
- 1/4 tsp black pepper, divided
- cooking spray
- 4 halibut fillets

Directions

- In a bowl, add the shallots, basil, cilantro, lemon juice, oil, 1/4 tsp of the salt and 1/8 tsp of the pepper and mix until well blended.
- Season the halibut fillets with the remaining salt and pepper evenly.
- Grease a grill pan with the cooking spray and heat over medium-high heat.
- Add the halibut fillets and cook for about 4 minutes per side.
- Place the chimichurri sauce over the halibut fillets and serve.

Servings Per Recipe: 4

Timing Information:

Preparation	20 mins
Total Time	30 mins

Nutritional Information:

Calories	401.3
Fat	10.2g
Cholesterol	190.8mg
Sodium	552.1mg
Carbohydrates	0.9g
Protein	71.8g

* Percent Daily Values are based on a 2,000 calorie diet.

Manioc Parmesan Bites
(Pao de Queijo)

Ingredients

- 2 C. sweet manioc starch
- 1 C. milk
- 1/2 C. margarine
- 1 tsp salt
- 1 1/2 C. grated parmesan cheese
- 2 eggs

Directions

- Before you do anything, preheat the oven to 400 F.
- Place a medium saucepan over medium heat. Stir in it the milk, salt, and margarine. Cook them until they start boiling.
- Turn off the heat. Stir in the starch into the milk mix until no lumps are found.
- Combine the eggs with cheese into the mix then mix them well with your hands until you get a soft dough.
- Shape the dough into 1 to 2 inches balls and place them on a lined up baking sheet.
- Cook the cheese bites in the oven for 8 to 14 min or until they become golden brown. Serve them hot with your favorite dip.
- Enjoy.

Servings Per Recipe: 1

Timing Information:

| Preparation | 20 mins |
| Total Time | 40 mins |

Nutritional Information:

Calories	87.8
Fat	7.6g
Cholesterol	26.9mg
Sodium	297.2mg
Carbohydrates	0.9g
Protein	3.9g

* Percent Daily Values are based on a 2,000 calorie diet.

Chicken Cutlets Chimichurri

Ingredients

- 4 large boneless skinless chicken breast halves
- 1 C. prepared chimichurri sauce
- 2 tbsp canola oil
- 1 medium red onion, peeled and cut into strips
- salt and pepper
- 4 sandwich buns, split
- nonstick cooking spray
- 4 slices Monterey Jack cheese
- 1 ripe avocado, sliced
- 1 C. lettuce leaf

Sauce:

- 2 C. loosely packed flat leaf parsley sprigs
- 1/2 C. loosely packed cilantro stem
- 1 Serrano Chile, coarsely chopped
- 2 tbsp red wine vinegar
- 1 tbsp minced garlic
- 1 1/4 tsp kosher salt
- 1/4 tsp pepper
- 1 C. olive oil

Directions

- For the chimichurri sauce: in a food processor, add the garlic, cilantro, parsley, Chile, vinegar, salt and pepper and pulse until finely chopped.
- While the motor is running, slowly add the oil and 1 tbsp of water and pulse until smooth nicely.
- For the chimichurri sandwiches: in a large zip lock bag, place the chicken and 3/4 C. of the chimichurri sauce.
- Seal the bag and shake to coat well.
- Refrigerate to marinate overnight.
- Set your grill for medium-high heat and lightly, grease the grill grate.
- Remove the chicken from bag and discard the marinade.
- Cook the chicken onto the grill for about 2-4 minutes per side.
- In the last minute of the cooking, place 1 cheese slice on top of each breast.
- Remove the chicken from the grill and keep aside for about 5 minutes.

- In a large skillet, heat the canola oil over medium heat and sauté the onion for about 8-10 minutes.
- Stir in the salt and pepper and remove from the heat.
- Place the remaining chimichurri sauce onto the cut side of each bun evenly.
- Top each bun with a chicken breast, followed by the onions, avocado and lettuce.
- Cover each with top bun and serve.

Servings Per Recipe: 4

Timing Information:

| Preparation | 4 hrs. |
| Total Time | 4 hrs. 15 mins |

Nutritional Information:

Calories	1007.7
Fat	82.0g
Cholesterol	100.4mg
Sodium	1065.2mg
Carbohydrates	31.4g
Protein	38.5g

* Percent Daily Values are based on a 2,000 calorie diet.

Porto Alegre Salsa

Ingredients

- 1 large onion, diced
- 1 large tomatoes, peeled, seeded and diced
- 2 tbsps red wine vinegar
- 2 garlic cloves, minced
- 1 -2 tbsp olive oil
- 1 tsp dried parsley
- 3 drops chili sauce
- salt, as needed
- pepper, as needed

Directions

- Get a large mixing bowl: Combine in it all the ingredients and stir them to coat.
- Place the sauce in the fridge for sit for at least 1 h. Serve it right away.
- Enjoy.

Servings Per Recipe: 2

Timing Information:

| Preparation | 10 mins |
| Total Time | 10 mins |

Nutritional Information:

Calories	112.4
Fat	7.0g
Cholesterol	0.0mg
Sodium	8.1mg
Carbohydrates	12.2g
Protein	1.7g

* Percent Daily Values are based on a 2,000 calorie diet.

Chimichurri Chicago Steak House

Ingredients

- 1 green bell pepper, stemmed seeded and quartered
- 2 mild chiles, stemmed seeded and quartered
- 1 jalapeño pepper, halved
- 1/4 C. parsley
- 2 garlic cloves
- 3 tbsp pepperoncini peppers, chopped
- 3 tbsp red wine vinegar
- salt

Directions

- In a food processor, add the bell pepper, jalapeño pepper and mild chilies and pulse until finely chopped.
- Add the remaining ingredients and pulse until slightly smooth.

Servings Per Recipe: 6

Timing Information:

Preparation	10 mins
Total Time	10 mins

Nutritional Information:

Calories	7.9
Fat	0.0g
Cholesterol	0.0mg
Sodium	52.0mg
Carbohydrates	1.7g
Protein	0.3g

* Percent Daily Values are based on a 2,000 calorie diet.

Rabanada

(Alternative French Toast)

Ingredients

- 1 medium sweet baguette
- 3 large eggs
- 3/4 C. sweetened condensed milk
- 6 tbsps whole milk
- 1/2 tsp vanilla extract
- 1/2 tsp kosher salt
- 1/2 C. granulated sugar
- 1 tbsp unsweetened cocoa powder
- 1/4 tsp ground cinnamon
- 3 -4 C. vegetable oil

Directions

- Slice the bread into 1 inch slices.
- Get a large mixing bowl: Mix in it the eggs, condensed milk, whole milk, vanilla extract, and salt. Whisk them well.
- Dip the bread slices completely in the eggs mix and cover the bowl with a piece of plastic wrap.
- Place a large pan over medium heat and heat 4 C. of vegetable oil in it.
- Drain the toast slices and cook them in the hot oil for 2 to 4 min on each side or until they become golden brown.
- Get a shallow dish: granulated sugar, cocoa powder and cinnamon. Coat the toast slices with the sugar mix then serve them warm.
- Enjoy.

Servings Per Recipe: 4

Timing Information:

Preparation	7 hrs
Total Time	7 hrs 15 mins

Nutritional Information:

Calories	1844.8
Fat	173.2g
Cholesterol	161.2mg
Sodium	436.4mg
Carbohydrates	67.5g
Protein	12.1g

* Percent Daily Values are based on a 2,000 calorie diet.

Chimichurri Mediterranean

Ingredients

- 8 garlic cloves, minced
- 1 tsp kosher salt
- 1 tsp oregano, dry leaves
- 1 tsp black pepper, ground
- 1 tsp red pepper flakes
- 3 lemons, zest
- 4 oz. lemon juice
- 1 bunch flat leaf parsley
- 1 C. olive oil

Directions

- In a food processor, add all the ingredients and pulse until just combined.
- Keep aside for about 30 minutes before serving.

Servings Per Recipe: 10

Timing Information:

| Preparation | 10 mins |
| Total Time | 10 mins |

Nutritional Information:

Calories	207.7
Fat	21.8g
Cholesterol	0.0mg
Sodium	182.5mg
Carbohydrates	4.2g
Protein	0.7g

* Percent Daily Values are based on a 2,000 calorie diet.

Brazilian Fruit Shots

Ingredients

- 2 tsps granulated sugar
- 1 lime
- 2 1/2 oz. cachaças
- 8 berries
- 1 -2 tbsp mango
- 1 -2 tbsp pineapple

Directions

- Place the lime wedges in a small mixing bowl. Sprinkle the sugar over the limes wedges and crush them with the back of a spoon.
- Spoon the mix to a cocktail shaker and to it the cachaça. Shake them well then pour the mix in a glassed filled with ice cubes.
- Serve your cocktail with your favorite toppings.
- Enjoy.

Servings Per Recipe: 1

Timing Information:

| Preparation | 10 mins |
| Total Time | 10 mins |

Nutritional Information:

Calories	213.1
Fat	0.1g
Cholesterol	0.0mg
Sodium	2.1mg
Carbohydrates	15.4g
Protein	0.4g

* Percent Daily Values are based on a 2,000 calorie diet.

Flank Steak del Barrio

Ingredients

- 1 tbsp olive oil
- 1/2 C. shallot, finely chopped
- 8 garlic cloves, minced
- 2 tbsp lemon juice
- 1 tbsp sherry wine vinegar
- 1/4 tsp crushed red pepper flakes
- 1 C. arugula, chopped
- 1/4 C. basil, finely chopped
- 1 tsp dried marjoram
- 3/4 tsp salt, divided
- 1/2 tsp pepper, divided
- 1/2 tsp smoked paprika
- 1 lb. flank steak
- cooking spray

Directions

- In a small nonstick skillet, heat the oil over medium-high heat and sauté the shallots and garlic for about 3 minutes.
- Remove from the heat and stir in the vinegar, lemon juice and red pepper.
- Keep aside to cool completely.
- Set your grill for medium-high heat and lightly, grease the grill grate.
- In a bowl, add the arugula, shallot mixture, marjoram, basil, 1/4 tsp of the salt and 1/4 tsp of the pepper and mix until well combined.
- In a small bowl, mix together the paprika, remaining salt and pepper.
- Rub the steak with the spice mixture evenly.
- Cook the steak onto the grill for about 6 minutes per side.
- Place the steak onto a cutting board for about 5 minute before slicing.
- Cut the steak into thin slices diagonally across the grain.
- Serve the steak slices with a topping of the sauce.

Servings Per Recipe: 4

Timing Information:

| Preparation | 15 mins |
| Total Time | 35 mins |

Nutritional Information:

Calories	245.8
Fat	12.9g
Cholesterol	77.1mg
Sodium	502.6mg
Carbohydrates	6.5g
Protein	25.2g

* Percent Daily Values are based on a 2,000 calorie diet.

COLLARD GREEN SKILLET

Ingredients

- 2 lbs collard greens
- 2 tbsps olive oil
- 1 tbsp butter
- 1/3 C. minced shallot
- 1 tbsp minced garlic
- kosher salt and pepper

Directions

- Remove the stems of the collard greens and slice them into thin strips.
- Place a large skillet over medium heat. Melt the butter in it. Sauté in it the garlic with shallot for 2 min.
- Stir in the collard greens and cook them for 12 to 14 min or until they are done. Adjust the seasoning of your stir fry then serve it warm.
- Enjoy.

Servings Per Recipe: 8

Timing Information:

Preparation	5 mins
Total Time	25 mins

Nutritional Information:

Calories	78.4
Fat	5.2g
Cholesterol	3.8mg
Sodium	31.8mg
Carbohydrates	7.0g
Protein	2.6g

* Percent Daily Values are based on a 2,000 calorie diet.

Chimichurri Aioli Glazed Tilapia

Ingredients

- 1/3 C. low-fat mayonnaise
- 2 tbsp lemon juice
- 1/3 C. diced onion
- 1 C. parsley
- 2 tbsp oregano
- 2 garlic cloves
- 8 tilapia fillets
- 2 tbsp Grated Parmesan Cheese

Directions

- Set your grill for medium heat and lightly, grease the grill grate.
- In a blender, add all the ingredients except the fish and cheese and pulse until well combined.
- In a bowl, add half of the mayo mixture and reserve it.
- Coat the tilapia fillets with the remaining mayo mixture evenly.
- Cook the tilapia fillets onto the grill for about 3 minutes per side.
- remove from the grill and immediately, top each fillet with the cheese.
- Serve the tilapia fillets alongside the reserved mayo mixture.

Servings Per Recipe: 8

Timing Information:

Preparation	10 mins
Total Time	20 mins

Nutritional Information:

Calories	7.9
Fat	0.0g
Cholesterol	0.0mg
Sodium	4.6mg
Carbohydrates	1.7g
Protein	0.3g

* Percent Daily Values are based on a 2,000 calorie diet.

South American Avocado Smoothie

Ingredients

- 1/2 avocado
- 1 1/2 C. milk
- 1/2 C. ice
- 3 tbsps sugar

Directions

- Get a food processor: Combine in it all the ingredients and blend them smooth.
- Serve your smoothie right away.
- Enjoy.

Servings Per Recipe: 1

Timing Information:

Preparation	5 mins
Total Time	6 mins

Nutritional Information:

Calories	541.3
Fat	28.1g
Cholesterol	51.2mg
Sodium	190.3mg
Carbohydrates	63.3g
Protein	14.0g

* Percent Daily Values are based on a 2,000 calorie diet.

Argentinian x Mexico Bake

Ingredients

- 1 (1 1/2 oz.) packets chimichurri seasoning
- 1 1/2 C. water
- 2 (8 oz.) cans tomato sauce
- 1 lb. ground beef
- 1 (15 oz.) cans black beans, rinsed and drained
- 1 (15 oz.) cans corn, drained
- 8 (8-inch) flour tortillas, warmed
- 1 1/2 C. Mexican blend cheese, shredded

Directions

- Set your oven to 350 degrees F before doing anything else and lightly, grease a 13x9-inch baking dish.
- In a bowl, add the tomato sauce, seasoning mix and water and mix until combined nicely.
- Heat a large skillet over medium-high heat and cook the beef until browned completely.
- Drain the grease from the skillet.
- Remove from the heat and stir in the beans, corn and 1 C. of the sauce mixture.
- Place about 1/2 C. of the beef mixture into each tortilla and carefully, fold like a burrito.
- Arrange the burritos into the prepared baking dish, seam side down.
- Spread the remaining sauce on top evenly, followed by the cheese.
- Cook in the oven for about 15 minutes.

Servings Per Recipe: 8

Timing Information:

| Preparation | 15 mins |
| Total Time | 40 mins |

Nutritional Information:

Calories	442.8
Fat	19.8g
Cholesterol	64.5mg
Sodium	811.5mg
Carbohydrates	44.0g
Protein	24.9g

* Percent Daily Values are based on a 2,000 calorie diet.

Brigadeiro (Mini Chocolate Truffles)

Ingredients

- 1 (14 oz.) cans sweetened condensed milk
- 1 tbsp butter
- 3 tbsps cocoa
- chocolate sprinkles

Directions

- Place a heavy saucepan over medium heat. Combine in it the condensed milk with cocoa powder and butter. Mix them well.
- Let them cook for 16 to 20 min until the mix becomes thick.
- Coat your palms with some butter and scoop some of the mix in your hands then shape it into a 1 1/2 inches balls. Place it on a lined up baking sheet.
- Repeat the process with the remaining mix to make more balls. Place them in the fridge to rest for at least 10 then serve them.
- Enjoy.

Servings Per Recipe: 40

Timing Information:

Preparation	5 mins
Total Time	20 mins

Nutritional Information:

Calories	35.9
Fat	1.1g
Cholesterol	4.1mg
Sodium	15.1mg
Carbohydrates	5.6g
Protein	0.8g

* Percent Daily Values are based on a 2,000 calorie diet.

Chipotle Parsley Halibut

Ingredients

- (6-oz) halibut fillets
- 1/4 C. shallot, diced
- 2 garlic cloves, minced
- 1 tbsp white wine vinegar
- 1 tbsp lemon juice, fresh
- 1 sprig thyme leave, chopped
- 1 sprig oregano, chopped finely
- 1/4 C. flat leaf parsley, fresh, chopped
- 1 tsp dried chipotle powder
- 1/4 C. extra virgin olive oil
- salt and pepper

Directions

- In a large bowl, add the shallots, garlic, lemon juice and vinegar and mix until well combined.
- Keep aside for about 30 minutes before using.
- In the bowl of the shallot mixture, add the herbs and mix until well combined.
- Add the oil and chipotle and ix until well combined.
- Add the halibut fillets and coat with the sauce generously.
- Refrigerate to marinate for at least 30 minutes.
- Remove the halibut fillets from the bowl and discard the marinade.
- Set your grill and lightly, grease the grill grate.
- Cook the halibut fillets onto the grill for about 2-3 minutes on each side.

Servings Per Recipe: 6

Timing Information:

Preparation	1 hr
Total Time	1 hr 4 mins

Nutritional Information:

Calories	278.8
Fat	11.8g
Cholesterol	102.8mg
Sodium	150.5mg
Carbohydrates	2.0g
Protein	39.0g

* Percent Daily Values are based on a 2,000 calorie diet.

Cod and Coconut Stew

Ingredients

- 1 lb fresh cod
- 2 limes, juice of
- 1 tsp salt
- 2 tbsps oil
- 2 onions, diced
- 1 bell pepper, diced (any color)
- 3 garlic cloves, minced
- 6 tomatoes, peeled seeded, diced
- 2 C. coconut milk
- 1 tsp Old Bay Seasoning
- pepper

Directions

- Get a large mixing bowl: Whisk in it the juice of 2 limes with a pinch of salt. Dip in it the cod fish and cover it with a plastic wrap. Place it in the fridge for 32 min.
- Place a large saucepan over medium heat. Heat the oil in it. Add the peppers with onion and cook them for 2 min. Stir in the garlic and cook them for 60 min.
- Stir in the tomato and cook them for 12 min. Add the fish with the coconut milk and old bay seasoning. Cook them until they start boiling.
- Lower the heat and cook the stew for 12 min. Serve it hot.
- Enjoy.

Servings Per Recipe: 2

Timing Information:

Preparation	15 mins
Total Time	30 mins

Nutritional Information:

Calories	1015.1
Fat	68.5g
Cholesterol	97.4mg
Sodium	1458.1mg
Carbohydrates	57.7g
Protein	53.5g

* Percent Daily Values are based on a 2,000 calorie diet.

Sonoma Black Bean Tacos

Ingredients

Brown Rice:

- 2 tbsp olive oil
- 1 onion, finely chopped
- 1/2 tsp sea salt
- 1 tomatoes, finely chopped
- 1/2 C. brown rice
- 1 C. vegetable broth

Sauce:

- 1 C. cilantro
- 1/2 C. Italian parsley
- 1/2 C. olive oil
- 1/4 C. lime juice
- 4 garlic cloves
- 2 tbsp agave syrup
- 1/2 tsp ground cumin
- 1 tsp sea salt
- 1/2 tsp ground black pepper

Filling:

- 2 tbsp olive oil
- 8 oz. cremini mushrooms, trimmed and sliced
- 1 (15 oz.) cans black beans, rinsed and drained
- 1 (8 oz.) packages flour tortillas

Finishing's:

- sour cream
- chopped tomato
- sliced onion
- shredded lettuce
- diced avocado

Directions

- For the tomato rice: heat the oil in a medium pan over medium-high heat and sauté the onions with the salt until tender.
- Stir in the rice, tomato and broth and bring to a rolling boil over high heat.
- Immediately, reduce the heat to low.
- Cover the pan and simmer until all the liquid absorbs.
- Remove from the heat and keep aside, covered for about 15 minutes.
- For the chimichurri sauce: in a food processor, add the garlic, parsley, cilantro, agave nectar, lime juice, oil, cumin, salt and pepper and pulse until well blended.

- In a small bowl, reserve half of the chimichurri sauce and keep aside.
- For the filling: heat the oil in a large skillet over medium-high heat and cook the mushrooms for about 3-4 minutes.
- Stir in the remaining chimichurri sauce and black beans and cook until heated completely.
- Place the tomato rice in each tortilla, followed by the mushroom mixture, reserved chimichurri sauce, your favorite topping and sour cream.
- Fold each tortilla like a burrito and serve.

Servings Per Recipe: 4

Timing Information:

| Preparation | 30 mins |
| Total Time | 1 hr 15 mins |

Nutritional Information:

Calories	764.7
Fat	46.3g
Cholesterol	0.0mg
Sodium	1249.8mg
Carbohydrates	74.6g
Protein	15.9g

* Percent Daily Values are based on a 2,000 calorie diet.

SAO PAULO POUNDCAKE

Ingredients

- 1/2 C. brazil nut
- 1/4 lb unsalted butter, softened
- 6 tbsps brown sugar, packed
- 3/4 C. flour
- 3 tbsps rice flour
- 1/2 tsp cinnamon

Directions

- Before you do anything preheat the oven to 325 F.
- Get a food processor: place in it the nuts and process them until they become finely ground.
- Get a mixing bowl: Beat in it the sugar with butter until they become light and fluffy.
- Add to them the ground nuts with flour and mix them well. Transfer the dough to a lined up baking sheet.
- Flatten it slightly with a rolling pin then use a sharp knife to prick on the sides to make 8 wedges without cutting them.
- Top the dough circle with some granulated sugar and cook it in the oven for 42 min.
- Allow your giant cookie to cool down completely then serve it.
- Enjoy.

Servings Per Recipe: 1

Timing Information:

| Preparation | 15 mins |
| Total Time | 1 hr 15 mins |

Nutritional Information:

Calories	254.7
Fat	17.4g
Cholesterol	30.5mg
Sodium	6.1mg
Carbohydrates	23.1g
Protein	2.8g

* Percent Daily Values are based on a 2,000 calorie diet.

Catfish Córdoba

Ingredients

- 1/2 C. parsley
- 1/2 C. basil
- 1/4 C. cilantro
- 1/4 C. olive oil
- 1 garlic clove, minced
- 1 tbsp red wine vinegar
- 2 tsp lime juice
- 1/4 tsp ground cumin
- 3/4 tsp salt, divided
- 1/4 tsp ground pepper
- 1 1/2 lb. catfish fillets
- 1/4 C. orange juice
- 1/2 tsp orange zest

Directions

- Set your oven to 425 degrees F before doing anything else and lightly, grease a baking dish.
- Sprinkle the catfish fillets with the orange zest, 1/2 tsp of the salt ad 1/8 tsp of the pepper.
- Arrange the catfish fillets into the prepared baking dish in a single layer and top with the orange juice evenly.
- Cook in the oven for about 12 minutes.
- Meanwhile, for the sauce: in a blender, add the garlic, cilantro, basil, parsley, vinegar, olive oil, lime juice, cumin, 1/4 tsp salt, 1/8 tsp pepper and pulse until smooth.
- Serve the catfish alongside the sauce.

Servings Per Recipe: 4

Timing Information:

Preparation	10 mins
Total Time	22 mins

Nutritional Information:

Calories	362.8
Fat	26.5g
Cholesterol	79.8mg
Sodium	531.8mg
Carbohydrates	3.0g
Protein	27.0g

* Percent Daily Values are based on a 2,000 calorie diet.

Sweet and Salty Raisin Rice

Ingredients

Rice

- 1 1/2 C. long-grain white rice
- 2 1/2 C. water (or more)
- 1/2 tsp salt
- 1 tbsp butter, unsalted

Spice

- 1 tbsp olive oil
- 3 slices turkey bacon, cut into strips
- 1/2 medium red onion, diced
- 1 garlic clove, peeled and minced
- 1/2 green bell pepper, diced
- 1/2 red bell pepper, diced
- 1/2 C. corn kernel, cooked
- 1/4 C. raisins, dark
- 1/4 C. raisins, golden
- 3 tbsps Italian parsley, chopped
- salt & pepper, to taste

Directions

- Place a large pot over medium heat. Rinse the rice and place it in it then add to it 2 1/2 C. of water.
- Add to it some butter with a pinch of salt. Cook it until it starts boiling. Put n the lid and lower the heat then let it cook for 22 min.
- Turn off the heat and let the rice rest for 6 min. Use a fork to fluff it and place it aside.
- Place a large skillet over medium heat. Heat the oil in it. Brown in it the bacon for 5 min. Drain it and place it aside.
- Reserve 2 tbsps of bacon fat in the skillet and discard the remaining of it. Stir in the onion, garlic, bell peppers, corn, both raisins, and the parsley.
- Let them cook for 6 min while stirring them from time to time. Add the rice and cook them for an extra 2 min.
- Adjust the seasoning of your rice skillet then serve it warm.
- Enjoy.

Servings Per Recipe: 4

Timing Information:

Preparation	15 mins
Total Time	45 mins

Nutritional Information:

Calories	441.7
Fat	9.9g
Cholesterol	11.7mg
Sodium	380.5mg
Carbohydrates	81.7g
Protein	8.0g

* Percent Daily Values are based on a 2,000 calorie diet.

Chimichurri Lettuce Appetizers

Ingredients

- 2 tbsp extra virgin olive oil
- 1 tbsp red wine vinegar
- 1 minced garlic clove
- 1 fresh jalapeño chili
- 2 tbsp oregano leaves
- 1/2 C. flat leaf parsley
- 8-12 oz. queso fresco
- 3 romaine lettuce hearts

Directions

- In a bowl, add all the ingredients except the queso fresco and lettuce and mix until well combined.
- Fold in the queso fresco.
- Arrange the romaine leaves onto a platter.
- Place the sauce onto each leaf and serve.

Servings Per Recipe: 8

Timing Information:

| Preparation | 20 mins |
| Total Time | 20 mins |

Nutritional Information:

Calories	72.9
Fat	4.1g
Cholesterol	0.0mg
Sodium	21.0mg
Carbohydrates	8.3g
Protein	3.0g

* Percent Daily Values are based on a 2,000 calorie diet.

Classic Dry Beef Chuck and Coconut Stew

Ingredients

- 3 lbs beef chuck, cut into 1 inch cubes
- 4 tbsps olive oil
- 6 large tomatoes, cut into wedges
- 1 large yellow onion, chopped
- 3 garlic cloves, minced
- 2 tsps fresh ginger, grated
- 1 (13 1/2 oz.) cans unsweetened coconut milk
- 1 tbsp dried oregano
- 1 tbsp red pepper flakes
- 1 tsp salt
- 1 tsp pepper
- 1 (19 oz.) cans black beans, drained and rinsed
- 1/3 C. fresh cilantro, chopped

Directions

- Place a large pan over high heat. Heat in it the olive oil. Brown in it the beef in batches for 5 min per batch.
- Stir the tomatoes, onion, garlic and ginger and cook them for 4 min. Add the coconut milk with oregano, red pepper flakes, salt and pepper.
- Cook them until they start boiling. Put on the lid and let them cook for 1 h 32 min while stirring them from time to time.
- Add the beans to the stew and let them cook for an extra 16 min. Adjust the seasoning of the stew and serve it warm.
- Enjoy.

Servings Per Recipe: 4

Timing Information:

| Preparation | 20 mins |
| Total Time | 2 hrs 20 mins |

Nutritional Information:

Calories	1386.4
Fat	102.6g
Cholesterol	234.7mg
Sodium	812.6mg
Carbohydrates	42.5g
Protein	76.3g

* Percent Daily Values are based on a 2,000 calorie diet.

Chimichurri Tilapia Cookout

Ingredients

- 2 whole tilapia fish
- aluminum foil
- 1 lemon, sliced
- 2 tsp seafood seasoning
- 2 tsp butter
- 1/4 C. flat-leaf Italian parsley, chopped
- 2 cloves, garlic, minced
- 1/2 tsp kosher salt
- 1/2 lemon, juiced
- 1/4 C. olive oil, extra virgin

Directions

- Set your grill for medium-high heat.
- Arrange each tilapia fish onto a greased square piece of foil.
- Sprinkle the cavity and sides of each tilapia with the seafood seasoning evenly.
- Arrange the lemon slices in the cavity of each tilapia and place the butter in the shape of dots.
- Seal the foil around each fish to make a parcel.
- Cook the parcels onto the grill for about 25 minutes.
- For the sauce: in a small bowl, add the garlic, parsley, garlic, lemon juice, oil and mix until well combined.
- Serve the fish alongside the sauce.

Servings Per Recipe: 4

Timing Information:

| Preparation | 10 mins |
| Total Time | 35 mins |

Nutritional Information:

Calories	147.9
Fat	15.5g
Cholesterol	5.0mg
Sodium	238.9mg
Carbohydrates	5.0g
Protein	0.8g

* Percent Daily Values are based on a 2,000 calorie diet.

SOUTH AMERICAN SEAFOOD SOUP

Ingredients

- 1 lb shrimp, peeled and veined
- 1/4 lb bay scallop
- 6 oz. white fish fillets, (cod fillet)
- 2 garlic cloves, minced
- 1/4 C. lemon juice
- 1 1/2 tsps salt
- 1/2 tsp black pepper
- 2 C. tomatoes, with juice
- 3/4 C. white onion
- 2 -3 limes, to make 1/4 c juice plus
- 1/2 C. red pepper, diced
- 1/2 C. green pepper, diced
- 1 jalapeno, seeded, diced
- 2 tbsps olive oil
- 1 (6 oz.) cans tomato paste
- 1/2 C. cilantro, chopped, divided
- 2 tsps fresh gingerroot
- 1/2 tsp crushed red pepper flakes (to taste)
- 1/4 tsp ground cayenne pepper
- 13 1/2 oz. unsweetened coconut milk

Directions

- Get a large mixing bowl: Stir in it the shrimp, scallops, fish ,garlic, lemon juice, 1/2 tsp salt and black pepper. Cover it with a plastic wrap and place it in the fridge for 22 min. Get a food processor: Combine in it the canned tomatoes with juices, 1/2 of cilantro, onions, jalapeno and 1/4 c lime juice. Blend them smooth and place it aside.
- Place a large pot over medium heat. Heat the oil in it. Sauté in it the red and green pepper with pepper flakes for 9 min.
- Add the rest of the cilantro, ginger, cayenne, and remaining salt. Sauté them for 1 min while stirring all the time.
- Stir in the tomato mix and cook them until they start boiling. Let them cook for 16 min over low heat.
- Add the tomato paste with coconut milk and bring them to another boil. Stir in the seafood and cook them again until they start boiling.
- Let the stew cook for 6 min. Adjust the seasoning of the stew then serve it warm. Enjoy.

Servings Per Recipe: 4

Timing Information:

Preparation	20 mins
Total Time	55 mins

Nutritional Information:

Calories	479.0
Fat	29.6g
Cholesterol	178.4mg
Sodium	2016.7mg
Carbohydrates	26.8g
Protein	32.4g

* Percent Daily Values are based on a 2,000 calorie diet.

Sopa de Papas con Chimichurri

Ingredients

- 2 stalks celery & leaves
- 2 tbsp prepared chimichurri sauce
- 1 (20 oz.) packages Simply Potatoes Diced Potatoes with Onion
- 3 C. milk
- 1 C. half-and-half

Directions

- Cut the celery stalk into 1/4-inch slices and then, mince the celery leaves finely.
- Add the sandwich spread in a large, heavy pan over medium heat and cook until heated through.
- Stir in the celery and celery leaves and cook until celery becomes crisp-tender.
- Add the potato package and stir to combine.
- Reduce the heat to medium-low and simmer for about 5 minutes, stirring frequently.
- Stir in the half-and half and milk and simmer, covered for bout 20-30 minutes or until desired doneness.
- Remove from the heat and serve immediately.

Servings Per Recipe: 6

Timing Information:

Preparation	10 mins
Total Time	55 mins

Nutritional Information:

Calories	132.6
Fat	9.1g
Cholesterol	32.0mg
Sodium	86.9mg
Carbohydrates	7.8g
Protein	5.2g

* Percent Daily Values are based on a 2,000 calorie diet.

RICE SKILLET WITH ORANGE AND PIMENTO

Ingredients

- 1 lb boneless chicken thighs, skinless, cut into 1/2 inch wide strips
- 1/4 C. olive oil
- 4 garlic cloves, finely chopped
- 1 tsp orange zest
- 1 1/2 C. water
- 1/2 C. orange juice
- 1 (8 oz.) packages yellow rice mix
- 1/2 C. pimento stuffed olive, halves
- 1 C. fresh cilantro, chopped
- orange wedge (to garnish)

Directions

- Season the chicken strips with a pinch of salt and pepper.
- Place a large pan over medium heat. Heat the oil in it. Brown in it the chicken with garlic and zest. Cook them for 4 min.
- Stir in 1 1/2 C. water and 1/2 C. orange juice. Cook them until they start boiling. Stir in the rice with seasoning packet, and olives.
- Cook them until they start boiling. Lower the heat and put on the lid. Let them cook for 20 min. Once the time is up, serve your chicken and rice skillet hot.
- Enjoy.

Servings Per Recipe: 4

Timing Information:

Preparation	20 mins
Total Time	50 mins

Nutritional Information:

Calories	378.6
Fat	30.9g
Cholesterol	95.3mg
Sodium	91.8mg
Carbohydrates	4.4g
Protein	20.1g

* Percent Daily Values are based on a 2,000 calorie diet.

South American Beef Kebabs

Ingredients

- 1/3 C. lemon juice
- 3 C. cilantro, packed
- 3 garlic cloves
- 1 tsp crushed red pepper flakes
- 1 tsp dried oregano
- 1 tsp kosher salt
- 1/2 C. vegetable oil
- 1 1/2 lb. sirloin steaks, cut into cubes
- 8 bamboo skewers, soaked in water for 30 minutes

Directions

- In a blender, add the garlic, cilantro, oil, lemon juice, oregano, pepper flakes and salt and pulse until pureed.
- In an airtight container, place about 2/3 C. of the sauce and reserve in the refrigerator.
- In a zip lock bag, add the beef cubes and remaining sauce and seal the bag after squeezing out the excess air.
- Shake the bag well to coat and refrigerator to marinate for at least 4 hours or overnight, shaking the bag occasionally.
- Set your grill for medium-high heat and lightly, grease the grill grate.
- Remove the beef cubes from the bag and discard the excess marinade.
- Thread the beef cubes onto pre-soaked skewers, leaving a little space.
- Season the beef cubes with the salt evenly.
- Cook the skewers onto the grill for about 3-4 minutes per side.
- Serve immediately alongside the reserved chimichurri sauce.

Servings Per Recipe: 4

Timing Information:

| Preparation | 4 hrs. |
| Total Time | 4 hrs. 8 mins |

Nutritional Information:

Calories	594.6
Fat	49.0g
Cholesterol	127.5mg
Sodium	530.8mg
Carbohydrates	2.8g
Protein	35.0g

* Percent Daily Values are based on a 2,000 calorie diet.

Brazilian Vegetarian Hot Pot (Ginger and Coconut Curry)

Ingredients

- 1 butternut squash, peeled and 2 cm dice
- 2 red onions, roughly chopped
- 1 aubergine, chopped
- 2 red peppers, diced
- 1 (400 g) cans chickpeas
- 2 garlic cloves, crushed
- 1/2 inch gingerroot, chopped
- 1 red chili pepper, deseeded and chopped
- 400 g chopped tomatoes
- 200 ml coconut cream
- 4 tbsps chopped fresh coriander
- 3 tbsps olive oil

Directions

- Before you do anything preheat the oven to 400 F.
- Get a large mixing bowl: Mix in it the veggies with 2 tbsps of oil. Spread the mix on a baking sheet and cook it for 42 min in the oven.
- Get a blender: Combine in it the chili, garlic, ginger and onion. Blend them smooth.
- Place a large pot over medium heat. Heat the rest of oil in it. Sauté in it the onion mix for 2 min. Stir in the tomato and cook it for 12 min.
- Stir in the coconut cream and let them cook for 6 min. Once the time is up, stir in the roasted veggies.
- Serve your curry hot.
- Enjoy.

Servings Per Recipe: 6

Timing Information:

Preparation	15 mins
Total Time	1 hr

Nutritional Information:

Calories	432.8
Fat	14.8g
Cholesterol	0.0mg
Sodium	230.9mg
Carbohydrates	72.8g
Protein	8.0g

* Percent Daily Values are based on a 2,000 calorie diet.

Italian Tomato Chimichurri

Ingredients

- 1/2 medium red onion, diced
- 1 bunch flat leaf parsley, chopped
- 2 Roma tomatoes, diced
- 5 garlic cloves, chopped
- 1/4 C. red wine vinegar
- 1/4 C. white vinegar
- 1/2 C. extra virgin olive oil
- 1/2 tsp salt
- 1/4 tsp black pepper
- 2 tbsp water

Directions

- In a bowl, add all the ingredients and mix until well combined.
- Refrigerate, covered for 2 hours tor up to overnight.

Servings Per Recipe: 6

Timing Information:

| Preparation | 15 mins |
| Total Time | 15 mins |

Nutritional Information:

Calories	179.9
Fat	18.2g
Cholesterol	0.0mg
Sodium	207.6mg
Carbohydrates	3.9g
Protein	1.0g

* Percent Daily Values are based on a 2,000 calorie diet.

BLACK BEAN STEW I

Ingredients

- 1 tbsp olive oil
- 1 stalk celery, small dice
- 2 carrots, peeled and small dice
- 2 medium onions, peeled and small dice
- 3 garlic cloves, peeled and minced
- 1 small red bell pepper, seeded and small dice
- 1 lb lean stewing beef, cut into 1/2 inch cubes
- 1 tsp ground cumin
- 1 tsp orange zest, Grated
- 1 (14 1/2 oz.) cans diced tomatoes, undrained
- 2 (14 1/2 oz.) cans black beans, drained and rinsed
- salt and pepper, to taste

Directions

- Place a large pot over medium heat. Heat the oil in it. Cook in it the celery, carrots, onions, garlic, and bell pepper with the lid on for 6 min.
- Stir in the cumin, orange zest and tomatoes. Let them cook for 32 min over low heat with the lid on.
- Once the time is up, add the black beans to pot. Let them cook for 28 min without covering the pot. Adjust the seasoning of the soup then serve it hot.
- Enjoy.

Servings Per Recipe: 6

Timing Information:

| Preparation | 20 mins |
| Total Time | 1 hr 24 mins |

Nutritional Information:

Calories	340.0
Fat	11.8g
Cholesterol	55.2mg
Sodium	69.0mg
Carbohydrates	33.1g
Protein	25.9g

* Percent Daily Values are based on a 2,000 calorie diet.

Cinnamon Cayenne Rib Eye Clásico

Ingredients

- 1 tsp smoked paprika
- 1 tsp cumin
- 1 tsp coriander seed
- 1/2 tsp garlic powder
- 1/2 tsp cayenne pepper
- 1/2 tsp cinnamon
- 1/2 tsp sea salt
- 1/2 tsp black pepper
- 1 tbsp canola oil
- 2 (14 oz.) rib eye steaks
- 2 C. Italian parsley
- 1/2 C. picked mint leaf, no stems
- 1/2 C. extra virgin olive oil
- 3 garlic cloves
- 2 tbsp lemon juice
- 1 pinch sea salt

Directions

- With a mortar and pestle, grind the coriander seeds, cumin, paprika, garlic powder, cayenne pepper, cinnamon, salt and black until coriander seeds are crushed and well combined.
- Season the steaks with the spice mixture generously.
- With a plastic wrap, cover the steaks and keep aside for about 20-30 minutes. Meanwhile, for the sauce: in a food processor, add the garlic, mint, parsley, lemon juice, olive oil, 1 tsp of the spice mixture and salt and pulse until smooth. Transfer the sauce into a container and refrigerate, covered until using.
- Set your grill for medium-high heat with the lid closed and lightly, grease the grill grate.
- Remove the plastic wrap from the steaks and coat them with the canola oil evenly.
- Cook the steaks onto the grill for about 2 minutes.
- Flip the steaks to 90 degrees and cook for about 2 minutes.
- Flip and cook for about 2-3 minutes.
- Place the steaks onto a cutting board for about 5 minutes before slicing. Cut the steaks into desired slices and serve alongside the sauce.

Servings Per Recipe: 4

Timing Information:

| Preparation | 20 mins |
| Total Time | 15 mins |

Nutritional Information:

Calories	839.9
Fat	74.9g
Cholesterol	134.9mg
Sodium	567.5mg
Carbohydrates	5.3g
Protein	36.2g

* Percent Daily Values are based on a 2,000 calorie diet.

Steak with Chimichurri

Ingredients

Chimichurri

- 1 bunch flat leaf parsley, leaves only
- 3 garlic cloves, peeled
- 3 tbsps red wine vinegar
- 1/2 lime, juice of, only
- 3 tbsps chopped oregano leaves
- 1 tsp ground cumin

Steak

- 1 tsp smoked paprika
- 120 ml extra virgin olive oil
- 1 red chili pepper, halved and seeded
- 1 (200 g) rib eye steaks
- 1 tbsp oil
- 1 bunch watercress
- cooked potato, sautéed with
- ground cumin

Directions

- To make the chimichurri:
- Get a blender: Combine in it all the chimichurri and blend them smooth. Adjust the seasoning of the sauce and place it aside.
- To make the rib eye steak:
- Coat the whole steak with oil then sprinkle over it some salt and pepper.
- Place a griddle pan over medium heat. Cook in it the steak for 2 to 4 min on each side.
- Serve your steak with watercress, potato, a pinch of cumin and the chimichurri sauce.
- Enjoy.

Servings Per Recipe: 1

Timing Information:

| Preparation | 10 mins |
| Total Time | 30 mins |

Nutritional Information:

Calories	1690.7
Fat	163.7g
Cholesterol	136.0mg
Sodium	202.2mg
Carbohydrates	20.6g
Protein	41.7g

* Percent Daily Values are based on a 2,000 calorie diet.

ARGENTINIAN OATMEAL FRIES

Ingredients

Fries:

- 6 tbsp white sesame seeds
- 1 C. cold cooked oatmeal
- 1/2 C. grated Parmigiano-Reggiano cheese

Sauce:

- 1 C. packed parsley leaves
- 1/4 C. packed cilantro leaves
- 2 garlic cloves, peeled
- 1/2 C. olive oil
- 1/3 C. red wine vinegar
- 3/4 tsp dried red pepper flakes
- 1/2 tsp ground cumin
- 1/2 tsp salt

Directions

- Heat a dry frying pan over medium heat and cook the sesame seeds until toasted, shaking the pan occasionally.
- Transfer the toasted sesame seeds onto a plate.
- Make 8 equal sized balls from the oatmeal.
- Coat each ball with the cheese and then roll into sesame seeds.
- With your hands, flatten each ball slightly.
- In a skillet, heat about 1/2-inch of vegetable oil over medium heat and cook the patties for about 10 minutes per side, pressing with the spatula slightly.
- Remove from the heat and immediately, sprinkle with the sea salt slightly.
- Meanwhile, for the sauce: in a food processor, add all the ingredients and pulse until smooth.
- Serve the fritters with a topping of the sauce.

Servings Per Recipe: 1

Timing Information:

Preparation	5 mins
Total Time	25 mins

Nutritional Information:

Calories	201.3
Fat	18.6g
Cholesterol	3.6mg
Sodium	282.7mg
Carbohydrates	5.7g
Protein	4.1g

* Percent Daily Values are based on a 2,000 calorie diet.

Fortaleza Stroganoff

Ingredients

- 2 lbs beef or 2 lbs chicken fillets, cut into 1 inch pieces
- 2 garlic cloves, minced
- 1 onion, chopped, divided
- salt
- 1/4 tsp nutmeg
- 1/2 tsp oregano
- 1/2 C. dry white wine
- 2 tbsps oil
- 1/2 lb cultivated white mushroom, sliced
- 2 -3 tbsps ketchup
- 1 1/2 tbsps mild mustard
- 1/2 C. sour cream

Directions

- Get a large mixing bowl: Combine in it the meat with garlic, half the onion, salt, nutmeg, oregano and wine. Toss them to coat. Let them sit for 1 h.
- Place a large skillet over medium heat. Heat the oil in it. Combine in it the rest of the onion with mushroom. Cook them for 4 min.
- Stir in the meat mix with mustard, ketchup and few tbsps of water. Let them cook for 8 to 12 min or until the meat is done.
- Once the time is up, stir in the cream. Heat the stew for 2 min then serve it hot.
- Enjoy.

Servings Per Recipe: 4

Timing Information:

| Preparation | 30 mins |
| Total Time | 50 mins |

Nutritional Information:

Calories	1707.3
Fat	173.9g
Cholesterol	239.6mg
Sodium	235.1mg
Carbohydrates	8.8g
Protein	21.8g

* Percent Daily Values are based on a 2,000 calorie diet.

Chimichurri Zucchini and Squash with Potatoes

Ingredients

- 16 small red potatoes
- 1/3 C. olive oil
- 1/4 C. red wine vinegar
- 1/2 tsp salt
- 3 garlic cloves, minced
- 1 C. parsley, chopped
- 1/4 C. cilantro, chopped
- 2 medium zucchini, sliced
- 2 medium yellow squash, sliced
- 1 small red onion, trimmed, peeled, and cut into wedges

Directions

- In a deep skillet, add the potatoes and enough water to cover over medium-high heat and bring to a boil.
- Reduce the heat to a medium-low and simmer for about 10 minutes.
- Drain the potatoes well and then, rinse them under cold running water.
- Add the vinegar, oil and salt in a bowl and beat until blended nicely.
- Add the garlic, cilantro and parsley and mix well.
- In a zip lock bag, place the vegetables and 3/4 of the chimichurri sauce.
- Seal the bag and shake to coat well.
- Refrigerate to marinate for about 30-60 minutes.
- Set your grill for medium-high heat and lightly, grease the grill grate.
- Thread the vegetables onto 8 (10-inch) metal skewers alternately.
- Cook the skewers onto the grill for about 6 minutes per side.
- Serve the skewers alongside the remaining chimichurri sauce.

Servings Per Recipe: 4

Timing Information:

Preparation	20 mins
Total Time	42 mins

Nutritional Information:

Calories	687.1
Fat	19.7g
Cholesterol	0.0mg
Sodium	440.2mg
Carbohydrates	117.6g
Protein	16.0g

* Percent Daily Values are based on a 2,000 calorie diet.

Brazilian Sausage

Ingredients

- 1 1/2 lbs linguica sausage
- 6 oz. coarsely grated cheese

Directions

- Before you do anything, preheat the grill and grease it.
- Cut each sausage in a half lengthwise. Grill the sausage slices for 4 min on each side.
- Adjust the sausages halves to make their open side facing up. Top them with the grated cheese and cook them for 4 min.
- Serve your cheesy sausages hot.
- Enjoy.

Servings Per Recipe: 8

Timing Information:

Preparation	0 mins
Total Time	10 mins

Nutritional Information:

Calories	70.5
Fat	5.2g
Cholesterol	13.6mg
Sodium	205.7mg
Carbohydrates	1.7g
Protein	4.1g

* Percent Daily Values are based on a 2,000 calorie diet.

Burgers Argentino

Ingredients

Sauce:

- 2 garlic cloves, peeled
- 1 jalapeño pepper, stemmed, halved and seeded
- 3/4 C. packed stemmed parsley leaves
- 1/2 C. olive oil
- 2 tbsp red wine
- 1/4 tsp salt
- 1 1/2 tsp dried oregano leaves
- 1/2 tsp dried red pepper flakes

Patties:

- 1 1/2 lb. lean ground beef
- salt
- fresh ground black pepper
- 4 oz. Gouda cheese, cubes
- 4 Kaiser rolls, split

Directions

- For the chimichurri sauce: in a food processor, add the jalapeño chile and garlic and pulse until finely minced.
- Add the parsley and pulse until finely minced.
- Add the vinegar, oil and salt and pulse until well blended.
- In a small bowl, add the sauce mixture and stir in the oregano and red pepper flakes. Keep aside for about 2 hours before using.
- For the burgers: set your barbecue grill for medium-high heat and lightly, grease the grill grate.
- In a large bowl, add the ground beef, 3 tbsp of the chimichurri sauce, salt and pepper and mix until well combined.
- Make 8 (5-inch) equal sized patties from the mixture.
- Place the cheese over 4 patties evenly.
- Cover with the remaining patties and press the edges to seal the cheese. Cook the patties onto the grill for about 5 minutes per side.
- In the last 1 minute of cooking, place the buns onto the grill, cut sides down. Place 1 patty in each bun and serve alongside the remaining chimichurri sauce.

Servings Per Recipe: 4

Timing Information:

Preparation	20 mins
Total Time	30 mins

Nutritional Information:

Calories	888.0
Fat	62.9g
Cholesterol	148.1mg
Sodium	808.0mg
Carbohydrates	32.7g
Protein	44.9g

* Percent Daily Values are based on a 2,000 calorie diet.

Spicy Pink Shrimp

Ingredients

- 1 1/2 lbs raw shrimp, peeled & deveined
- 1/4 C. olive oil
- 1/4 C. onion, diced
- 1 garlic clove, minced
- 1/4 C. roasted red pepper, diced
- 1/4 C. fresh cilantro, chopped
- 14 oz. diced tomatoes
- 1 C. coconut milk
- 2 tbsps sriracha sauce
- 2 tbsps fresh lime juice
- salt and pepper

Directions

- Place a large saucepan over medium heat. Heat the oil in it.
- Cook in it the onion for 3 min. Stir in the garlic with peppers for another 3 min.
- Stir in the tomatoes, shrimp and cilantro. Cook them for 4 min.
- Stir in the coconut milk and Sriracha sauce. Cook them for 3 min. Stir in the lime juice with a pinch of salt and pepper. Serve your stew warm.
- Enjoy.

Servings Per Recipe: 6

Timing Information:

Preparation	20 mins
Total Time	50 mins

Nutritional Information:

Calories	352.1
Fat	18.2g
Cholesterol	143.2mg
Sodium	1007.2mg
Carbohydrates	31.1g
Protein	16.6g

* Percent Daily Values are based on a 2,000 calorie diet.

Orzo Calabasas

Ingredients

- 4 garlic cloves, peeled
- 1/2 C. cilantro leaf
- 1/2 C. Italian flat leaf parsley
- 1/4 C. onion, chopped
- 1 poblano pepper, halved, seeded and chopped
- 2 tbsp lime juice
- 1 tsp salt
- 1/4 C. olive oil
- fresh ground black pepper
- 1 (16 oz.) packages orzo pasta
- 1 red bell pepper, quartered, seeded and diced

Directions

- In a food processor, with steel knife blade, add the onion, garlic, poblano, parsley, cilantro, lime juice and salt and pepper and pulse until pureed.
- While the motor is running, slowly add the oil and pulse until well combined.
- In a large pan, add the water and salt and bring to a boil.
- Add the orzo and cook as directed by the package.
- Drain the orzo well and transfer into a bowl.
- Add the bell pepper and sauce and toss to coat well.
- Serve immediately.

Servings Per Recipe: 8

Timing Information:

Preparation	10 mins
Total Time	35 mins

Nutritional Information:

Calories	287.8
Fat	7.8g
Cholesterol	0.0mg
Sodium	297.9mg
Carbohydrates	46.1g
Protein	8.1g

* Percent Daily Values are based on a 2,000 calorie diet.

Potato Salad Brazilian II

Ingredients

- 5 -6 medium white rose potatoes
- 1 medium apple, peeled cored and finely diced
- 1 C. carrot, cooked till tender but not mushy, diced into small cubes
- 1 C. frozen peas, lightly blanched and cooled
- 1 C. frozen corn kernels, defrosted
- 1 C. mayonnaise, to taste
- 1/2 C. sliced pimento-stuffed green olives
- salt and pepper, to taste

Directions

- Get a large mixing bowl: Mix in it all the ingredients.
- Adjust the seasoning of the salad and serve it right away.
- Enjoy.

Servings Per Recipe: 10

Timing Information:

Preparation	20 mins
Total Time	20 mins

Nutritional Information:

Calories	211.8
Fat	8.1g
Cholesterol	6.1mg
Sodium	197.9mg
Carbohydrates	32.8g
Protein	3.7g

* Percent Daily Values are based on a 2,000 calorie diet.

Ginger Honey Glazed Kebabs

Ingredients

- 500 g beef, ground
- 1 onion
- 1/4 C. pine nuts, toasted
- 1 small hot pepper, deseeded and finely minced
- 3 garlic cloves, finely minced
- 1 slice bread, soaked in water, squeezed dry and crumbled
- 1 egg yolk
- salt and pepper
- 1 tsp sweet paprika
- 1/4 tsp cumin
- 1/4 tsp baking soda
- 3 tbsp olive oil

Honey Glaze:

- 1/4 C. date honey
- 1/4 C. balsamic vinegar
- 1 tbsp ginger, finely minced
- 1 tbsp brown sugar
- 1/4 C. beef broth
- salt and pepper

Sauce:

- 1 bunch parsley, coarsely minced
- 1/2 C. olive oil
- 1 small hot pepper, deseeded
- 1/4 C. white vinegar
- 3 -5 garlic cloves
- salt and pepper

Directions

- For the kebabs: in a bowl, add the ground beef, onion, garlic, bread slice and pine nuts and mix until well combined.
- In another bowl, add the olive oil, egg yolk, baking soda and spices and beat well.
- Add the egg yolk mixture into the bowl of the beef mixture and with your hands, knead until well combined.
- Keep aside for a few minutes.
- With greased hands, make small balls from the beef mixture.
- Shape each ball into kebab and freeze for a few minutes.
- Set your oven to 450 degrees F and lightly, grease a baking sheet.

- Arrange the kebabs onto the prepared baking sheet and cook in the oven for about 10-15 minutes.
- For the ginger sauce: in a pan, add all the ingredients and bring to a boil.
- Cook until the desired thickness of the sauce is achieved.
- For the chimichurri: in a food processor, add all the ingredients except the oil and pulse until well combined.
- While the motor is running, slowly add the oil and pulse until well combined.
- Serve the kebabs alongside the both sauces.

Servings Per Recipe: 16

Timing Information:

Preparation	20 mins
Total Time	35 mins

Nutritional Information:

Calories	167.0
Fat	16.0g
Cholesterol	17.2mg
Sodium	49.9mg
Carbohydrates	4.6g
Protein	1.6g

* Percent Daily Values are based on a 2,000 calorie diet.

BRASILEIRO SKIRTS

Ingredients

- 1 whole skirt steak
- sea salt (enough to coat steak)

Directions

- Season the steak with some salt on both sides.
- Place a pan over medium high heat. Grease it and cook in it the steak for 2 to 4 mi on each.
- You can grill it also or bake it for 26 min on 350 F. Serve it warm.
- Enjoy.

Servings Per Recipe: 2

Timing Information:

Preparation	8 mins
Total Time	48 mins

Nutritional Information:

Calories	371.9
Fat	18.6g
Cholesterol	147.4mg
Sodium	151.9mg
Carbohydrates	0.0g
Protein	47.8g

* Percent Daily Values are based on a 2,000 calorie diet.

Chiang Mai x Houston Chimichurri

Ingredients

- 3/4 C. bottled green chili salsa
- 1/4 C. unsweetened coconut milk
- 1 green onion, chopped
- 1/2 tsp shredded lime peel
- 1 tbsp lime juice
- 1 tbsp chopped cilantro
- 1 tbsp chopped of mint
- 1 tsp green curry paste
- 1 tsp grated ginger
- 1 tsp soy sauce
- 1 garlic clove, minced
- 4 boneless skinless chicken breast halves
- chopped mango
- chopped cucumber
- mint

Directions

- For the sauce: in a food processor, add the salsa, green onion, garlic, ginger, mint, cilantro, lime peel, coconut milk, lime juice, soy sauce and curry paste and pulse until smooth.
- In a bowl, add 1/3 C. of the sauce and preserve in refrigerator until using.
- In a large zip lock bag, place the chicken and remaining marinade.
- Seal the bag and shake to coat well.
- Refrigerate to marinate for about 1-2 hours, shaking the bag often.
- Set your charcoal grill for medium heat and lightly, grease the grill grate.
- Remove the chicken from the bag, reserving the marinade.
- Place the chicken onto the grill directly over coals and cook for about 12-15 minutes, flipping once and coating with the reserved marinade halfway through.
- Transfer the chicken onto a platter and drizzle with the reserved sauce.
- Serve with a garnishing of the mint alongside the mango and cucumber.

Servings Per Recipe: 4

Timing Information:

Preparation	10 mins
Total Time	10 mins

Nutritional Information:

Calories	176.0
Fat	4.5g
Cholesterol	68.4mg
Sodium	455.1mg
Carbohydrates	4.5g
Protein	28.6g

* Percent Daily Values are based on a 2,000 calorie diet.

AMBROSIA PUDDING

Ingredients

- 6 eggs
- 1/2 C. orange juice
- 2 tbsps orange zest, grated
- 1/2 lb sugar

Directions

- Before you do anything, preheat the oven to 300 F.
- Get a mixing bowl: Whisk in it all the ingredients. Pour the mix through a fine mesh sieve to strain it.
- Pour the batter in a greased 8/6 inches ceramic dish. Cook the pudding in the oven for 22 min. serve it with your favorite toppings after it cools down.
- Enjoy.

Servings Per Recipe: 4

Timing Information:

Preparation	10 mins
Total Time	30 mins

Nutritional Information:

Calories	343.5
Fat	7.2g
Cholesterol	279.0mg
Sodium	107.4mg
Carbohydrates	61.2g
Protein	9.6g

* Percent Daily Values are based on a 2,000 calorie diet.

Chimichurri Shrimp

Ingredients

- 18 large shrimp
- 1 1/2 lb. skirt steaks

Sauce:

- 6 garlic cloves
- 2/3 C. olive oil
- kosher salt & ground pepper
- 2 tbsp red wine vinegar
- 1 bunch flat leaf parsley, top leaves only
- 2 tbsp oregano leaves
- 1 lemon, juice

Directions

- For the chimichurri sauce: in a food processor, add all the ingredients and pulse until smooth.
- Transfer the chimichurri sauce into a large glass bowl.
- Add the steak and shrimp and coat with the chimichurri sauce generously.
- Refrigerate to marinate for about 1/2-1 hour.
- Set your grill for high heat and lightly, grease the grill grate.
- Place the steak onto the grill and cook for about 5 minutes.
- Flip the steak and coat with some extra chimichurri sauce.
- Coat the shrimp and coat with some extra chimichurri sauce.
- Now, place the shrimp onto the grill with the steak and cook until desired doneness.
- Transfer the steak and onto a platter.
- With a sharp knife, cut the steak into thin slices diagonally across the grain.
- Serve the steak and shrimp alongside the extra chimichurri sauce.

Servings Per Recipe: 6

Timing Information:

Preparation	1 hr
Total Time	1 hr 12 mins

Nutritional Information:

Calories	481.5
Fat	35.9g
Cholesterol	98.7mg
Sodium	130.6mg
Carbohydrates	3.3g
Protein	35.4g

* Percent Daily Values are based on a 2,000 calorie diet.

HABANERO RICE

Ingredients

- 1 tbsp vegetable oil
- 1 small onion, finely diced
- 1 garlic clove, minced
- 1 C. long-grain rice
- 1 habanero pepper
- 2 -2 1/4 C. hot water
- 1/2 tsp salt

Directions

- Place a pot over medium heat. Heat the oil in it. Cook in it the rice with garlic and onion for 5 min.
- Stir in the chili pepper, hot water, and salt. Cook them until they start boiling.
- Let the rice cook for 18 to 22 min or until the rice is done. Let it sit for 5 min the fluff it with a fork.
- Discard the hot pepper and serve your rice warm.
- Enjoy.

Servings Per Recipe: 4

Timing Information:

Preparation	5 mins
Total Time	35 mins

Nutritional Information:

Calories	211.4
Fat	3.7g
Cholesterol	0.0mg
Sodium	298.3mg
Carbohydrates	39.8g
Protein	3.7g

* Percent Daily Values are based on a 2,000 calorie diet.

Burgers Brasileiro

Ingredients

- 1 tbsp ground cumin
- 1 C. cilantro leaves
- 1 C. Italian parsley
- 2 tbsp champagne vinegar
- 1 tsp crushed red pepper flakes
- 1/2 tsp coarse salt
- 1/4 C. canola oil
- 2 lb. lean ground beef
- 1/4 tsp salt
- 1/4 tsp ground red pepper
- 6 rolls, Mexican bolitos, split and toasted
- 1 tomatoes, sliced
- 1 onion, sliced
- 6 plantains, peeled and cut into slices

Directions

- Set your grill for medium heat and lightly, grease the grill grate.
- Heat a small frying pan over low heat and cook the cumin for about 2 minutes, stirring continuously.
- Immediately, remove from the heat.
- For the chimichurri sauce: in a blender, add the parsley, cilantro, vinegar, cumin, red pepper and salt and pulse on lowest speed until well combined.
- While the motor is running, slowly add the oil and pulse until well combined.
- In a large bowl, add the ground beef, 1/4 tsp of the salt and ground red pepper and mix until well combined.
- Make (3 1/2-inch) 12 patties in from the beef mixture.
- In the center of each of 6 patties, place 1 tbsp of the chimichurri sauce.
- Cover each with the remaining patty and press the edges to seal the filling.
- Arrange the patties onto the grill directly over the heat and cook for about 18-22 minutes, flipping once halfway through.
- Transfer the patties onto a platter and cover with a piece of foil to keep warm.
- Coat the plantain slices with the peanut oil evenly.

- Arrange the plantain slices onto the grill directly over medium heat and cook for about 8 minutes, flipping once halfway through.
- Remove from the grill and transfer the plantain slices onto a paper towel-lined plate to drain.
- Spread a thin layer of the chimichurri sauce onto each roll and top with the burgers, followed by the remaining sauce, tomatoes and onions.
- Serve the burgers alongside the plantain slices.

Servings Per Recipe: 6

Timing Information:

Preparation	30 mins
Total Time	48 mins

Nutritional Information:

Calories	750.6
Fat	27.6g
Cholesterol	98.2mg
Sodium	717.4mg
Carbohydrates	90.9g
Protein	39.0g

* Percent Daily Values are based on a 2,000 calorie diet.

FEIJOADA II
(FULL BLACK BEAN STEW)

Ingredients

- 1 1/2 lbs small black turtle beans, soaked for an overnight
- 1/2 lb brazilian dried beef
- 1 ham hock
- 1 lb pork ribs
- 1 lb smoked chorizo sausage
- 1 lb beef sirloin
- 1/2 lb slab smoked bacon
- 1/2 lb smoked pig (optional)
- 1/4 C. vegetable oil
- 2 onions, finely chopped
- 3 garlic cloves, mashed
- 1/3 C. parsley, chopped
- 1 1/2 tsps cumin
- 1 bay leaf
- salt and pepper, to taste

Directions

- Place a large pot over medium heat. place in it the beans and cover it with water.
- Stir in the ham hock with dry beef. Cook them for 2 h. Once the time is up, discard the ham hock.
- Add the smoked bacon with sirloin, pork ribs, and bay leaf to the beans pot. Let them cook for 32 min.
- Place a large pan over medium heat. Heat the oil in it. Sauté in it the garlic with onion for 3 min.
- Stir in the parsley with cumin, a pinch of salt and pepper. Cook them for 1 min.
- Stir in 3/4 C. of beans mix and mash them with a fork. Pour the mix into the beans pot and cook them for an extra 30 min.
- Drain the meats and slice them then place them on a serving plate. Drain the beans serve it with some white rice along with the meats.
- Enjoy.

Servings Per Recipe: 8

Timing Information:

Preparation	15 hrs
Total Time	18 hrs

Nutritional Information:

Calories	2536.5
Fat	170.5g
Cholesterol	834.8mg
Sodium	2651.0mg
Carbohydrates	5.5g
Protein	230.6g

* Percent Daily Values are based on a 2,000 calorie diet.

COUNTRY SIRLOIN ARGENTINIAN

Ingredients

- 1 1/2 lb. sirloin steaks, trimmed
- 1 1/2 C. cilantro stems
- 1 C. white vinegar
- 3/4 C. chopped onion
- 2 tsp ground cumin
- 2 tsp dried thyme
- 2 tsp cracked black pepper
- 1 tsp kosher salt
- 6 minced garlic cloves
- 3 bay leaves
- cooking spray
- chimichurri sauce

Directions

- In a large re-sealable bag, add all the ingredients except the cooking spray and chimichurri sauce.
- Seal the bag and shake well to coat completely.
- Refrigerate to marinate for about 3 hours, shaking the bag occasionally.
- Set your grill for medium heat and lightly, grease the grill grate.
- Remove the steak from the bag and discard the marinade.
- Cook the steak onto the grill for about 8 minutes per side.
- Transfer the steak onto a cutting board for about 3 minutes before slicing.
- With a sharp knife, cut the steak into thin slices diagonally across the grain.
- Serve the steak slices alongside the chimichurri sauce.

Servings Per Recipe: 2

Timing Information:

| Preparation | 10 mins |
| Total Time | 26 mins |

Nutritional Information:

Calories	1192.2
Fat	78.4g
Cholesterol	333.2mg
Sodium	1130.1mg
Carbohydrates	13.8g
Protein	97.6g

* Percent Daily Values are based on a 2,000 calorie diet.

BRASILEIRO FLANK

Ingredients

- 2 lbs flank steaks
- 6 garlic cloves, minced
- 1/2 small hot pepper
- 2 tsp extra virgin olive oil
- 1/4 tsp kosher salt
- 1 (14 oz) cans hearts of palm, drained, halved lengthwise and thinly sliced
- 4 medium tomatoes, chopped
- 1/2 C. red onion, chopped
- 1/2 small hot chili peppers
- 1/4 C. fresh cilantro, chopped
- 2 tbsp red wine vinegar
- 1/4 tsp kosher salt

Directions

- Before you do anything preheat the grill.
- Get a small mixing bowl: Mix in it the garlic, hot pepper, oil and salt. Coat the whole steak with the mix.
- Grease the grill and cook in it the steak for 5 to 7 min on each side.
- Get a small mixing bowl: Toss in it the hearts of palm, tomatoes, onion, hot pepper, cilantro, vinegar and salt to make the salsa.
- Cover the steak with a piece of foil and let it sit for 6 min. Serve it with the tomato salsa.
- Enjoy.

Servings Per Recipe: 4

Timing Information:

Preparation	30 mins
Total Time	50 mins

Nutritional Information:

Calories	464.2
Fat	21.9g
Cholesterol	154.2mg
Sodium	772.7mg
Carbohydrates	13.6g
Protein	52.4g

* Percent Daily Values are based on a 2,000 calorie diet.

Chimichurri Route-66

Ingredients

- 1 (27 oz.) cans tender green cactus pieces, in brine, drained
- 1/2 C. olive oil
- 1 garlic clove
- 1/2 lemon, juice
- 1/2 lime, juice
- 1 pinch red pepper flakes
- salt & pepper
- cilantro

Directions

- In a food processor, add the cactus, garlic, cilantro, red pepper flakes, salt, pepper and juice of lime and lemon and pulse until chopped finely.
- While the motor is running, slowly add the oil and pulse until well combined.

Servings Per Recipe: 10

Timing Information:

Preparation	5 mins
Total Time	10 mins

Nutritional Information:

Calories	97.1
Fat	10.8g
Cholesterol	0.0mg
Sodium	0.3mg
Carbohydrates	0.4g
Protein	0.0g

* Percent Daily Values are based on a 2,000 calorie diet.

Lime Glazed Sirloin

Ingredients

- 4 sirloin steaks, 1 1/2-inches thick
- 1/2 C. lime juice, freshly squeezed
- 1/3 C. dry red wine
- 1 small onion, finely chopped
- 4 garlic cloves, finely chopped
- 2 tsp dried oregano
- 1 bay leaf
- 1 tsp coarse salt
- 1 tsp black pepper

Sauce

- 5 malgueta bell peppers
- 1 tsp salt
- 1 small white onion, finely diced
- 4 large garlic cloves, chopped
- 3 limes, juice of
- 1/2 bunch Italian parsley, chopped

Directions

- Get a food processor: Combine in it the sauce ingredients and process them until they become smooth to make the sauce. Place it aside.
- Lay the steaks on a roasting pan and place it aside.
- Get a small mixing bowl: Mix in it the lime juice with red wine, onion, garlic, oregano, bay leaf, salt and pepper to make the marinade.
- Coat the steaks completely with the marinade and place them in the fridge for at least 4 h.
- Before you do anything preheat the grill and grease it.
- Drain the steaks and cook them for 7 to 9 min on each side. Serve your steaks warm with lime sauce.
- Enjoy.

Servings Per Recipe: 4

Timing Information:

Preparation	15 mins
Total Time	30 mins

Nutritional Information:

Calories	1311.3
Fat	77.6g
Cholesterol	456.0mg
Sodium	1488.8mg
Carbohydrates	18.9g
Protein	125.9g

* Percent Daily Values are based on a 2,000 calorie diet.

Fish with Tropical Mango Chimichurri

Ingredients

- 1 C. mango
- 1/2 C. red bell pepper, seeded, ribs discarded, chopped
- 1/2 C. cilantro, chopped
- 1/2 C. parsley, chopped
- 1/4 C. lime juice
- 3 tbsp white wine vinegar
- 1 tbsp garlic, minced
- 1 tbsp dried oregano
- 2 tsp jalapeños, chopped
- sea salt
- ground black pepper
- 1 tbsp olive oil
- 1 lb. red snapper filets, cut into cubes, or white fish filets
- 1 (14 oz.) cans black beans, drained
- 1 C. cooked long grain brown rice, warm
- 4 flour tortillas

Directions

- In a large bowl, add the mango, bell pepper, garlic, parsley, cilantro, jalapeño, vinegar, lime juice, oregano, 1/4 tsp of the salt and 1/4 tsp of the black pepper and mix well.
- Season the snapper fillets with 1/4 tsp of the salt and 1/4 tsp of the black pepper.
- In a large nonstick skillet, heat the oil over medium-high heat and cook the snapper fillets for about 5 minutes, flipping occasionally.
- Stir in the rice and beans and cook for about 1-2 minutes.
- Remove from the heat and stir in the mango mixture.
- Place the snapper mixture onto each tortillas evenly.
- Wrap each tortilla and serve.

Servings Per Recipe: 4

Timing Information:

Preparation	15 mins
Total Time	25 mins

Nutritional Information:

Calories	578.4
Fat	9.7g
Cholesterol	53.2mg
Sodium	266.4mg
Carbohydrates	79.3g
Protein	43.2g

* Percent Daily Values are based on a 2,000 calorie diet.

Goya Recaito and Seafood Stew

Ingredients

- 2 tbsp olive oil
- 1 onion, chopped fine
- 4 C. chicken stock
- 4 tbsp goya recaito
- 2 tbsp tomato paste
- 14 oz coconut milk
- 12 littleneck clams
- 12 mussels
- 1/2 lb large shrimp
- 2 lobster tails, snipped in half lengthwise before serving
- red pepper, stripped
- green pepper, stripped
- fresh cilantro
- lemon wedge
- lime wedge
- chili oil

Garnishes

Directions

- Place a large saucepan over medium heat. Heat some oil in it. Cook in it the onion for 6 min.
- Stir in the stock, cilantro cooking base, tomato paste and coconut milk. Bring them to a boil. Lower the heat and put on the lid. Let them cook for 22 min.
- Stir in the seafood put on the lid. Let them cook for 6 min. Serve your seafood warm.
- Enjoy.

Servings Per Recipe: 4

Timing Information:

Preparation	20 mins
Total Time	50 mins

Nutritional Information:

Calories	496.8
Fat	30.5g
Cholesterol	121.8mg
Sodium	705.1mg
Carbohydrates	24.8g
Protein	32.2g

* Percent Daily Values are based on a 2,000 calorie diet.

AMERICAN-MESA CHIMICHURRI

Ingredients

- 1/2 C. chopped cilantro
- 3/4 C. chopped Italian parsley
- 3 garlic cloves
- 1/2 C. red wine vinegar
- 1/3 C. olive oil
- 1 Serrano pepper
- 1/2 tsp cracked black pepper
- 1/2 tsp cumin
- 1 tsp season salt

Directions

- In a food processor, add all the ingredients and pulse until smooth.

Servings Per Recipe: 4

Timing Information:

| Preparation | 15 mins |
| Total Time | 15 mins |

Nutritional Information:

Calories	168.9
Fat	18.1g
Cholesterol	0.0mg
Sodium	8.6mg
Carbohydrates	1.9g
Protein	0.6g

* Percent Daily Values are based on a 2,000 calorie diet.

Brazilian Long Grain II

Ingredients

- 1 tbsp butter
- 1 C. white rice
- salt

Directions

- Place a large saucepan over medium heat. Heat 1 tbsp of butter in it.
- Stir in the rice and cook it for 3 min. Stir in 2 C. of water with a pinch of salt. Bring it to a boil.
- Put on the cover and let it cook for 16 min over medium heat. Turn off the heat and let it sit for 6 min. Serve it warm.
- Enjoy.

Servings Per Recipe: 3

Timing Information:

Preparation	0 mins
Total Time	20 mins

Nutritional Information:

Calories	262.1
Fat	4.1g
Cholesterol	10.1mg
Sodium	38.1mg
Carbohydrates	50.3g
Protein	4.2g

* Percent Daily Values are based on a 2,000 calorie diet.

Chimichurri Havana

Ingredients

- 7 garlic cloves, peeled
- 1 1/4 C. packed cilantro leaves
- 3/4 C. packed parsley sprig
- 1 tsp crushed red pepper flakes
- 1 tsp coarse ground black pepper
- 1/4 C. white balsamic vinegar
- 2 tbsp lime juice
- 1 tbsp soy sauce
- 1/2 tsp lime zest
- 1/3 C. olive oil
- grilled steak

Directions

- In a small food processor, add the garlic, parsley, cilantro, pepper flakes and pepper and pulse until finely chopped.
- Add the soy sauce, lime juice, vinegar and lime peel and pulse until well combined.
- While the motor is running, slowly add the oil and pulse until well combined.
- Serve the steak alongside the sauce.

Servings Per Recipe: 8

Timing Information:

| Preparation | 20 mins |
| Total Time | 20 mins |

Nutritional Information:

Calories	89.3
Fat	9.0g
Cholesterol	0.0mg
Sodium	130.8mg
Carbohydrates	2.0g
Protein	0.6g

* Percent Daily Values are based on a 2,000 calorie diet.

Garlicky Chicken with Mango Salsa

Ingredients

- 8-10 garlic cloves, finely chopped
- salt
- fresh ground black pepper
- 1 lemon, juice and zest of, divided
- 1/2 C. fresh parsley, chopped
- 2-3 dashes hot sauce
- 4 boneless skinless chicken breasts
- 1 large ripe mango, pitted and chopped
- 4 plum tomatoes, seeded and chopped
- 1/2 medium red onion, chopped
- 1/4 C. cilantro, chopped
- 1 lime, juice of
- 1 C. all-purpose flour
- 2 eggs
- 1/2 C. dried breadcrumbs
- 1/2 C. grated Parmigiano-Reggiano cheese
- 2-3 dashes nutmeg
- 2 tbsp extra virgin olive oil

Directions

- Before you do anything, preheat the oven to 250 F.
- Get a food processor: Combine in it the garlic with lemon juice, parsley, hot sauce, a pinch of salt and pepper. Process them several times until they become finely chopped.
- Place the chicken breasts on a working surface and use a kitchen hammer to flatten them until they become 1/4 inch thick.
- Coat the chicken breasts with the garlic mix and place them in the fridge for 12 min.
- Get a small mixing bowl: Toss in it the mango, plum tomatoes, red onion, cilantro, lime juice, some salt and freshly ground black pepper.
- Get a shallow bowl: Whisk in it the eggs with 1 tsp of water.
- Get another mixing bowl: Mix in it the breadcrumbs, grated Parmigiano-Reggiano, nutmeg and lemon zest.

- Place a large pan over medium heat. Heat 2 tbsp of oil in it.
- Dust the chicken breasts with some flour and dip them in the beaten eggs then coat them with the cheese and breadcrumbs mix.
- Cook the chicken breasts in the hot oil for 5 to 6 min on each side. Serve your chicken breasts warm.
- Enjoy.

Servings Per Recipe: 4

Timing Information:

| Preparation | 20 mins |
| Total Time | 40 mins |

Nutritional Information:

Calories	509.5
Fat	14.8g
Cholesterol	181.3mg
Sodium	392.4mg
Carbohydrates	52.8g
Protein	40.9g

* Percent Daily Values are based on a 2,000 calorie diet.

6-Ingredient Steak with Mock Chimichurri

Ingredients

- 1 C. A 1 garlic & herb marinade
- 2 C. parsley sprigs
- 1/3 C. olive oil
- 2 tbsp red wine vinegar
- 1 bay leaf
- 1 tsp dried oregano leaves

Directions

- In a large bowl, add the steak and marinade and mix well.
- Refrigerate for at least 30 minutes.
- Set the broiler of your oven and arrange oven rack about 4-inch from the heating element. Grease a rack, arrange in a broiler pan.
- Meanwhile, for the sauce: in a blender, add the remaining ingredients and pulse until smooth.
- Transfer the sauce into a bowl and refrigerate before using.
- Remove the steak from the bowl and discard the marinade.
- Arrange the steak onto the prepared rack and cook under the broiler for about 5 minutes per side.
- Transfer the steak onto a cutting board for about 5 minutes.
- Cut the steak into thin slices diagonally across the grain.
- Serve the steak slices alongside the sauce.

Servings Per Recipe: 8

Timing Information:

| Preparation | 15 mins |
| Total Time | 1 hr 10 mins |

Nutritional Information:

Calories	86.2
Fat	9.1g
Cholesterol	0.0mg
Sodium	8.9mg
Carbohydrates	1.1g
Protein	0.4g

* Percent Daily Values are based on a 2,000 calorie diet.

BRAZILIAN SHRIMP SKILLET

Ingredients

- 20 -30 tiger shrimp
- 2 onions, diced
- 1 green pepper, diced
- 2 tomatoes, diced
- 1 C. chopped fresh cilantro
- 20 oz unsweetened coconut milk
- 5 tbsp palm oil
- salt and pepper
- steamed white rice

Directions

- Place a large skillet over medium heat. Heat the palm oil in it. Sauté in it the prawns for 4 min.
- Stir in the coconut milk, salt, pepper and half the cilantro. Let them cook for 4 min.
- Once the time is up, serve your shrimp skillet warm with some white rice or noodles.
- Enjoy.

Servings Per Recipe: 4

Timing Information:

| Preparation | 20 mins |
| Total Time | 30 mins |

Nutritional Information:

Calories	512.5
Fat	49.0g
Cholesterol	45.6mg
Sodium	70.9mg
Carbohydrates	13.9g
Protein	10.4g

* Percent Daily Values are based on a 2,000 calorie diet.

Roasted Peppermint Roast

Ingredients

- 2-3 lb. well-trimmed tri-tip roast
- 1/4 C. lime juice
- 2 tbsp olive oil
- 1/4 C. minced cilantro
- 1 tbsp minced green onion
- 2 garlic cloves, minced
- 1 tbsp minced peppermint
- 1/2 tbsp ground pepper
- 2 tbsp sugar
- salt

Directions

- In a large re-sealable bag, add the roast, green onion, garlic, mint, cilantro, oil and lime juice.
- Seal the bag and shake to coat well.
- Refrigerate for about 2 hours.
- Set your smoker for an indirect temperature between 225 and 250°F.
- Arrange the roast with the marinade in the center of a foil piece of foil.
- Wrap the foil around the meat loosely to make a pouch.
- Cook the wrapped meat in smoker for about 3 hours.
- Remove the meat from the foil pouch and cook in the smoker for about 30 minutes, flipping once halfway through.
- Transfer the meat onto a cutting board.
- Cut the meat into desired sized pieces.
- Carefully, place the foil juice into a skillet over medium heat.
- Add the sugar and pepper and cook until the mixture reduced by half.
- Stir in the meat pieces and remove from the heat.
- Serve hot.

Servings Per Recipe: 8

Timing Information:

Preparation	2 hrs.
Total Time	6 hrs.

Nutritional Information:

Calories	46.4
Fat	3.4g
Cholesterol	0.0mg
Sodium	0.8mg
Carbohydrates	4.3g
Protein	0.1g

* Percent Daily Values are based on a 2,000 calorie diet.

Latin Flavored Butter

Ingredients

- 1/2 C. unsalted butter, softened
- 2 tsp sugar
- 2 oz orange juice
- 1 orange, zest of
- 1 lemon, zest of
- 2 tbsp Grand Marnier, orange liquor, optional

Directions

- Bring a large saucepan of water to a boil. Cook in it the orange and lemon zest for 2 min. Drain them and finely chop them.
- Get a large mixing bowl: Combine in it all the ingredients. Beat them until they become smooth and creamy. Place the butter in the fridge until ready to serve.
- Enjoy.

Servings Per Recipe: 10

Timing Information:

| Preparation | 10 mins |
| Total Time | 15 mins |

Nutritional Information:

Calories	87.3
Fat	9.2g
Cholesterol	24.4mg
Sodium	1.3mg
Carbohydrates	1.4g
Protein	0.1g

* Percent Daily Values are based on a 2,000 calorie diet.

Eliza's Chimichurri

Ingredients

- 1 C. flat leaf parsley, chopped fine
- 1/2 C. cilantro, chopped fine
- 2 tbsp thyme, stemmed and chopped fine
- 1/2 C. white onion, minced
- 1 C. extra virgin olive oil
- 1 tbsp garlic, minced
- 2 tbsp lemon juice
- 1 tbsp lime juice
- 2 tsp kosher salt
- 1/2 tsp cumin
- 1 tsp ground black pepper

Directions

- Add all the ingredients in a food processor and pulse until smooth.
- Transfer the sauce into a bowl and refrigerate, covered for at least 1 hour or up to three days.

Servings Per Recipe: 1

Timing Information:

Preparation	10 mins
Total Time	10 mins

Nutritional Information:

Calories	1334.4
Fat	144.6g
Cholesterol	0.0mg
Sodium	2358.0mg
Carbohydrates	14.0g
Protein	2.6g

* Percent Daily Values are based on a 2,000 calorie diet.

Catalina's Comfort Cake

Ingredients

- 4 large egg yolks
- 1 C. sugar, divided
- 12 oz cream cheese, at room temp
- 1 1/2 C. heavy cream, well-chilled
- 1 C. rum, optional
- 10 1/2 oz ladyfingers
- 2 C. ripe mangoes, diced
- 2 C. fresh ripe pineapple, diced
- 2 C. ripe papayas, diced
- extra mango
- extra pineapple
- extra papaya

Directions

- Get a large mixing bowl: Mix in it the egg yolks and 2/3 C. sugar until they become pale and creamy.
- Place the bowl on a double boiler and keep mixing it for 5 min until the mix becomes thick. Place the batter aside and let it cool down completely.
- Get a blender: Pour in it the egg batter with the cream cheese. Blend them smooth until they become light and creamy.
- Get a large mixing bowl: Beat in it the heavy cream until it soft peaks. Fold it into the eggs batter. Place it in the fridge until ready to use.
- Place a small saucepan over medium heat. Stir in it the liquor with the remaining 1/3 C. sugar. Let them cook for 6 min. Place it aside to cool down completely to make the syrup.
- Place the ladyfingers in the syrup then drain them and place 1/3 of them in a serving glass dish. Top it with the mango and 1/3 of the cream mix.
- Lay on them 1/3 of the ladyfingers followed by pineapple and 1/3 of the cream mix. Repeat the process using papaya this time.
- Place the cream bowl in the fridge for at least 3 h. Serve it with your favorite toppings.
- Enjoy.

Servings Per Recipe: 8

Timing Information:

| Preparation | 30 mins |
| Total Time | 12 hrs 30 mins |

Nutritional Information:

Calories	685.8
Fat	37.0g
Cholesterol	282.6mg
Sodium	216.8mg
Carbohydrates	66.0g
Protein	9.4g

* Percent Daily Values are based on a 2,000 calorie diet.

Buenos Aires Brisket

Ingredients

Sauce:

- 7 garlic cloves, peeled
- 4 jalapeño peppers, seeded and chopped
- 7 bay leaves
- 1 1/4 C. flat leaf parsley
- 2/3 C. cilantro leaf
- 2 1/2 tbsp dried oregano
- 1 1/4 C. distilled white vinegar
- kosher salt
- 2 C. water

Beef:

- 3 1/2 lb. beef brisket, soaked in cold water to cover for 1 hour, drained

Directions

- For the chimichurri: in a food processor, add the jalapeños, garlic and bay leaves and pulse until chopped finely.
- Add the cilantro, oregano and parsley and pulse until chopped finely.
- While machine running, add the oil and vinegar and pulse until smooth. Add the salt and pulse to combine.
- Transfer 1 C. of the chimichurri into a container and refrigerate, covered until using.
- In a large ceramic baking dish add the water and remaining chimichurri and mix until well combined.
- Add the brisket and coat with the marinade generously.
- With a plastic wrap, cover the baking dish and refrigerate for about 24-48 hours. Set your oven to 350 degrees F and arrange a rack in the center of the oven. In a roasting pan, place the brisket with marinade.
- Cover the roasting pan and cook in the oven for about 3 1/2 hours.
- Remove from the oven and place the brisket onto a cutting board to cool slightly before slicing. Cut the brisket into desired sized slices diagonally. Meanwhile, in a microwave-safe bowl, add the reserved chimichurri and microwave until heated slightingly.
- Serve the brisket slices alongside the chimichurri sauce.

Servings Per Recipe: 6

Timing Information:

| Preparation | 45 mins |
| Total Time | 4 hrs. 15 mins |

Nutritional Information:

Calories	851.4
Fat	70.5g
Cholesterol	193.1mg
Sodium	180.6mg
Carbohydrates	3.4g
Protein	45.7g

* Percent Daily Values are based on a 2,000 calorie diet.

Summer Night Banana Coffee Smoothie

Ingredients

- 1 C. skim milk
- 1 tsp cinnamon
- 2 medium bananas
- 2 C. coffee ice cubes
- Splenda sugar substitute, to taste (optional)

Directions

- Get a food processor: combine in it all the ingredients and blend them smooth.
- Serve your coffee shake.
- Enjoy

Servings Per Recipe: 2

Timing Information:

Preparation	5 mins
Total Time	5 mins

Nutritional Information:

Calories	158.6
Fat	0.7g
Cholesterol	2.4mg
Sodium	73.8mg
Carbohydrates	34.8g
Protein	6.2g

* Percent Daily Values are based on a 2,000 calorie diet.

Picnic Chimichurri

Ingredients

- 6 garlic cloves, peeled
- 1 C. packed flat-leaf parsley
- 1 C. packed cilantro
- 3 green onions
- 1/4 C. oregano leaves
- 1 jalapeño, stem removed
- 1 tbsp kosher salt
- 1 tbsp black pepper
- 1 tsp red pepper flakes
- 1 tbsp smoked paprika
- 1 C. extra virgin olive oil
- 1/2 C. red wine vinegar
- 1/4 C. water
- 2 limes, juiced

Directions

- In a food processor, add all the ingredients and pulse until well combined.
- In a 1 gallon re-sealable bag, place the meat and chimichurri and seal the bag after squeezing out the excess air.
- Refrigerate for about 6-7 hours, shaking the bag often.
- Remove the meat from the bowl and discard the marinade.
- Keep the meat at the room temperature for about 20-30 minutes before cooking.
- Cook the meat onto grill until cooked through.

Servings Per Recipe: 1

Timing Information:

| Preparation | 7 hrs. |
| Total Time | 7 hrs. |

Nutritional Information:

Calories	2129.4
Fat	220.7g
Cholesterol	0.0mg
Sodium	7044.9mg
Carbohydrates	51.7g
Protein	9.5g

* Percent Daily Values are based on a 2,000 calorie diet.

Savory Pineapple Steaks

Ingredients

- 1 C. brown sugar
- 2 tsp ground cinnamon
- 1 pineapple, peeled, cored, and cut into 6 wedges

Directions

- Before you do anything preheat the grill and grease it.
- Get a small mixing bowl: Mix in it the brown sugar and cinnamon.
- Get a large zip lock bag: Place in it the pineapple slices with the sugar mix. Seal the bag and shake it to coat them.
- Place the pineapple slices on the grill and cook them for 4 to 6 min on each side. Serve them with some ice cream.
- Enjoy.

Servings Per Recipe: 6

Timing Information:

Preparation	10 mins
Total Time	20 mins

Nutritional Information:

Calories	216.9
Fat	0.1g
Cholesterol	0.0mg
Sodium	11.8mg
Carbohydrates	56.4g
Protein	0.8g

* Percent Daily Values are based on a 2,000 calorie diet.

Manhattan Strip Steaks

Ingredients

- 4 (12 oz.) New York strip steaks
- salt & pepper

Sauce:

- 1 C. Spanish olive oil
- 2 limes, juice
- 4 garlic cloves
- 2 shallots, minced
- 1 tbsp basil, minced
- 1 tbsp thyme
- 1 tbsp oregano leaves
- salt and pepper

Directions

- For the chimichurri marinade: in a bowl, add all the ingredients and mix until well combined.
- In a large baking dish, add the steaks and half of the chimichurri marinade mix well.
- Refrigerate, covered for about 2 hours.
- Set your grill for high heat and lightly, grease the grill grate.
- Remove the steaks from the refrigerator and keep aside in room temperature for about 20 minutes before cooking.
- Remove the steak from the bowl and discard the marinade.
- Sprinkle each steak with the salt and pepper evenly.
- Cook the steaks onto the grill for about 4-5 minutes per side.
- Remove the steaks from the grill and place onto a platter for about 10 minutes before serving.
- Serve the steaks alongside the remaining chimichurri sauce.

Servings Per Recipe: 4

Timing Information:

Preparation	15 mins
Total Time	30 mins

Nutritional Information:

Calories	1271.2
Fat	106.7g
Cholesterol	275.5mg
Sodium	180.2mg
Carbohydrates	4.7g
Protein	70.7g

* Percent Daily Values are based on a 2,000 calorie diet.

Brazilian Wild Rice

Ingredients

- 6 oz wild rice
- 3/4 C. dry vermouth
- 1/4 C. butter
- 3 tbsp onions, finely chopped
- 1/2 liter mushroom
- 2 eggs, well beaten (optional)
- salt and pepper

Directions

- Before you do anything, preheat the oven to 350 F.
- Prepare the rice according to the directions on the package. Fluff the rice and add to it the dry vermouth. Mix them well.
- Place a heavy saucepan over medium heat. Heat the butter in it until it melts. Sauté in it the onion for 3 min.
- Stir in the mushroom and cook them for 6 min. Add the rice with eggs, a pinch of salt and pepper. Mix them well.
- Pour the mix in a greased casserole dish. Cook it it in the oven for 32 min. Serve your casserole warm.
- Enjoy.

Servings Per Recipe: 4

Timing Information:

| Preparation | 10 mins |
| Total Time | 1 hr 10 mins |

Nutritional Information:

Calories	312.2
Fat	12.1g
Cholesterol	30.5mg
Sodium	108.8mg
Carbohydrates	37.2g
Protein	8.0g

* Percent Daily Values are based on a 2,000 calorie diet.

Red Pepper Rib-Eye with Balsamic Chimichurri

Ingredients

- 1/2 C. packed chopped cilantro
- 6 tbsp balsamic vinegar
- 2 tbsp olive oil
- 2 garlic cloves, peeled and minced
- 1 tsp adobo seasoning
- 1/2 tsp dried oregano
- 1/2 tsp pepper
- 1/4 tsp dried red chili pepper flakes
- 2 boned beef rib eye steaks
- 2 tsp steak herb seasoning mix
- 2 tbsp butter

Directions

- For the chimichurri sauce: in a bowl, add the garlic, cilantro, oil, vinegar, oregano, adobo seasoning, pepper, and chile flakes and mix until well combined.
- Rub each steak with the seasoning mix evenly.
- In a 10-12-inch nonstick frying pan, melt 1 tsp of the butter over medium-high heat and cook the steaks for about 10 minutes, flipping frequently.
- Place the steaks onto a platter and cover with a piece of foil to keep warm.
- In the same pan, melt the remaining butter and stir in the chimichurri sauce.
- Cut each steak into 2 equal sized pieces.
- Arrange the steak pieces onto the serving plates.
- Transfer any meat juices from the platter into the frying pan and combine it with the sauce.
- Pour the sauce mixture over the steak pieces and serve.

Servings Per Recipe: 4

Timing Information:

Preparation	15 mins
Total Time	30 mins

Nutritional Information:

Calories	135.9
Fat	12.5g
Cholesterol	15.2mg
Sodium	60.3mg
Carbohydrates	5.0g
Protein	0.3g

* Percent Daily Values are based on a 2,000 calorie diet.

LATIN LEEKS WITH SWEET VINAIGRETTE

Ingredients

- 4 leeks
- 4 -6 tbsp olive oil
- 1/2 tbsp unsalted butter
- kosher salt & freshly ground black pepper, to taste

Vinaigrette:

- 1/2 C. balsamic vinegar, good quality
- 5 tsp sugar

Directions

- Place a heavy saucepan over medium heat: Whisk in it the balsamic vinegar and sugar. Heat it until it dissolves.
- Cook the mix until it starts simmering. Keep cooking it for 8 min until it reduces by 4 tbsp at least.
- Slice the leeks in half lengthwise and rinse them well. Slice them into strips.
- Place a large pan over medium heat. Heat the butter with oil in it. Sauté in it the leeks for 16 to 20 min.
- Serve your butter leek with the sweet vinegar.
- Enjoy.

Servings Per Recipe: 4

Timing Information:

| Preparation | 20 mins |
| Total Time | 50 mins |

Nutritional Information:

Calories	234.7
Fat	15.2g
Cholesterol	3.8mg
Sodium	25.6mg
Carbohydrates	23.2g
Protein	1.5g

* Percent Daily Values are based on a 2,000 calorie diet.

Brazilian Casserole (Shrimp, Corn, and Parmesan and Peppers)

Ingredients

- 2 tbsp virgin olive oil
- 1/2 C. chopped yellow onion
- 1/4 C. chopped green bell pepper
- 1 lb fresh jumbo shrimp, cleaned and deveined
- 2 tbsp chopped fresh parsley
- 1/4 C. canned tomato sauce
- 2 tbsp mild salsa
- 1 tsp salt
- 1 tsp fresh ground black pepper
- 2 tbsp all-purpose flour
- 1 C. milk
- 1 tbsp vegetable shortening, for greasing the baking dish
- 2 C. canned cream-style corn
- 1/2 C. grated parmesan cheese

Directions

- Before you do anything, preheat the oven to 375 F.
- Place a large pan over medium heat. Heat the oil in it. Sauté in it the bell pepper with onion for 4 min.
- Stir in the shrimp and parsley. Let them cook for 3 min. Add the tomato sauce, salsa, salt, and pepper. Lower the heat and let them cook for 6 min with the lid on.
- Add the flour followed by the milk gradually while stirring all the time. Turn the heat to medium an let them cook for 4 min.
- Turn off the heat and place the stew aside to cool down for a while.
- Pour the stew in a greased casserole dish. Spread the cream corn over it then top them with the parmesan cheese.
- Place the casserole in the oven and let it cook for 28 min. Once the time is up, serve it hot.
- Enjoy.

Servings Per Recipe: 6

Timing Information:

| Preparation | 0 mins |
| Total Time | 45 mins |

Nutritional Information:

Calories	256.0
Fat	11.7g
Cholesterol	108.3mg
Sodium	1277.5mg
Carbohydrates	22.8g
Protein	17.0g

* Percent Daily Values are based on a 2,000 calorie diet.

Cumin Coriander Flank Steak

Ingredients

- 1 1/2 lb. flank steaks

Spice Mix:

- 1 1/2 tsp kosher salt
- 1/2 tsp ground coriander
- 1/2 tsp ground cumin
- 1/4 tsp black pepper

Sauce:

- 2 cloves garlic, minced
- 1 1/2 C. cilantro
- 1 1/2 C. flat leaf parsley
- 1/4 C. white vinegar
- 1/3 C. olive oil
- 1/4 tsp cayenne

Directions

- Set the broiler of your oven and arrange oven rack about 4-inch from the heating element.
- For the rub: in a bowl, add all the ingredients and mix well.
- Rub the steak with the rub mixture generously.
- Cook the steak under the broiler for about 6 minutes on both sides.
- Meanwhile, for the chimichurri sauce: add all the ingredients in a food processor and pulse until finely chopped.
- Remove the steak from the oven and place onto a cutting board for about 5 minutes.
- With a sharp knife, cut the steak into thin slices diagonally.
- Serve alongside the chimichurri sauce.

Servings Per Recipe: 4

Timing Information:

Preparation	10 mins
Total Time	25 mins

Nutritional Information:

Calories	456.8
Fat	32.4g
Cholesterol	115.6mg
Sodium	763.2mg
Carbohydrates	2.6g
Protein	37.0g

* Percent Daily Values are based on a 2,000 calorie diet.

Brazilian Potatoes

Ingredients

- 2 lbs small baby potatoes
- 3/4 C. good quality olive oil
- 1/3 C. red wine vinegar
- 1 tsp dried oregano
- 2 -3 garlic cloves, minced
- kosher salt & freshly ground black pepper
- 1/2 C. chopped white onion
- 1 -2 tsp finely minced chili pepper (or to taste)
- 1 C. olive, pitted
- 1/4 C. diced sun-dried tomato
- 1/4 C. chopped parsley

Directions

- Bring a large salted pot of water to a boil. Cook in it the potato until they become soft. Drain them and place them aside.
- Get a large mixing bowl: Mix in it the olive oil, red wine vinegar, oregano, garlic, and salt and pepper. Add the potato and stir them to coat.
- Place the bowl aside until the potato cools down completely. Add to it the onions, chili pepper, olives, sun dried tomatoes, and chopped parsley. Mix them well.
- Place the salad in the fridge for at least 1 h then serve it.
- Enjoy.

Servings Per Recipe: 6

Timing Information:

Preparation	6 hrs
Total Time	6 hrs 25 mins

Nutritional Information:

Calories	385.4
Fat	29.6g
Cholesterol	0.0mg
Sodium	239.7mg
Carbohydrates	28.3g
Protein	3.3g

* Percent Daily Values are based on a 2,000 calorie diet.

Rosario Chimichurri

Ingredients

- 6 garlic cloves, minced
- 2 shallots, minced
- 2 C. parsley, minced
- 1/4 C. oregano leaves, minced
- 1 tbsp salt
- 1 tsp red pepper flakes
- 1 C. olive oil
- 1/2 C. red wine vinegar
- 1/4 C. water

Directions

- In a bowl, add all the ingredients and with a whisk, mix until well combined.
- Any kind of meat or veggies can be marinated in his sauce.

Servings Per Recipe: 1

Timing Information:

Preparation	5 mins
Total Time	5 mins

Nutritional Information:

Calories	1040.5
Fat	109.8g
Cholesterol	0.0mg
Sodium	3530.4mg
Carbohydrates	17.7g
Protein	4.1g

* Percent Daily Values are based on a 2,000 calorie diet.

Thursday's Latin Lunch Box Salad

Ingredients

- 1 lettuce
- 2 C. pineapple, crunches
- 1/4 C. onion, sliced
- 1 lb tomatoes
- 1/2 C. celery, chopped

Sauce

- 1/2 C. plain nonfat yogurt
- 1/4 C. olive oil
- 1 lime, juice of
- salt and pepper

Garnish

- 1/2 C. peanuts, rough chopped

Directions

- Get a food processor: Combine in it the sauce ingredients and blend them smooth.
- Get a large mixing bowl: Mix in it all the salad ingredients. Add to it the sauce and toss them to coat.
- Serve your salad with some peanuts or your other favorite toppings.
- Enjoy.

Servings Per Recipe: 4

Timing Information:

Preparation	15 mins
Total Time	15 mins

Nutritional Information:

Calories	310.6
Fat	22.9g
Cholesterol	0.6mg
Sodium	44.6mg
Carbohydrates	22.8g
Protein	8.1g

* Percent Daily Values are based on a 2,000 calorie diet.

Lemon Lime Skirt Steak with Chimichurri

Ingredients

Skirt:

- 1 tsp garlic, minced
- 1 tsp cilantro leaf, chopped
- 2 tbsp olive oil
- 3 tbsp tequila
- 1 tbsp lemon juice, squeezed
- 1 tbsp lime juice, freshly squeezed
- 1/2 tsp salt
- 1 tsp black pepper, cracked
- 1 1/2 lb. skirt steaks, trimmed

Sauce:

- 2 tbsp cilantro leaves, chopped
- 2 tbsp parsley leaves, chopped
- 1 tbsp basil leaves, chopped
- 1 tbsp oregano leaves, chopped
- 2 tbsp white onions, minced
- 2 tbsp red bell peppers, diced
- 2 tbsp garlic, minced
- 1 tsp salt
- 1 tbsp black pepper, cracked
- 1/2 tsp ground cumin
- 2 tbsp red wine vinegar
- 1 tbsp dried pasilla pepper
- 2 tbsp extra virgin olive oil

Directions

- For the steak: in a large bowl, add all the steak and mix until well combined.
- Add the steak and oat with the marinade generously.
- Refrigerate to marinate for about 1-3 hours.
- Meanwhile, for the chimichurri sauce: in a food processor, add all the ingredients and gently, stir to combine.
- Transfer the sauce into a bowl and keep aside for about 2 hours before serving.
- Set your grill for high heat and lightly, grease the grill grate.

- Remove the steak from the bowl and discard the marinade.
- Cook the steak onto the grill for about 5-10 minutes or until desired doneness.
- Remove the steak from the grill and place onto a cutting board.
- Cut the steak into 1/4-inch pieces against the grain.
- Serve the steak pieces with a topping of the chimichurri sauce.

Servings Per Recipe: 4

Timing Information:

Preparation	2 hrs. 30 mins
Total Time	2 hrs. 40 mins

Nutritional Information:

Calories	488.6
Fat	30.8g
Cholesterol	100.3mg
Sodium	1007.2mg
Carbohydrates	4.9g
Protein	46.3g

* Percent Daily Values are based on a 2,000 calorie diet.

Kielbasa Stew

Ingredients

- 1 lb beef stew meat, seasoned with salt and pepper
- 1 tbsp vegetable oil
- 8 oz kielbasa, sliced into 1/2 inch thick rounds
- 1/4 C. orange juice
- 1 1/2 C. diced onions
- 1 (14 1/2 oz) cans diced tomatoes
- 1 (15 oz) cans black beans, drained and rinsed
- 1 (15 oz) cans black beans, drained and rinsed and pureed
- 2 tbsp minced garlic
- 1 tbsp chili powder
- 1 tbsp red wine vinegar
- sliced jalapeno
- orange wedge
- orange zest

Directions

- Place a large pan over high heat. Heat the oil in it. Cook in it the stew meat in batches for 6 min until it browned. Drain it and place it aside.
- Cook the kielbasa in the same pan for 4 min per batch. Drain it and placei it aside.
- Stir the orange juice in the same pan to deglaze it.
- Stir the onions, tomatoes, beans, garlic, and chili powder in a slow cooker. Add to it the stew meat with orange juice, beans, a pinch of salt and pepper.
- Put on the lid and cook the stew on high for 5 h.
- Once the time is up, stir in the vinegar. Serve your stew hot.
- Enjoy.

Servings Per Recipe: 6

Timing Information:

| Preparation | 30 mins |
| Total Time | 4 hrs 30 mins |

Nutritional Information:

Calories	409.8
Fat	16.9g
Cholesterol	73.2mg
Sodium	429.9mg
Carbohydrates	34.5g
Protein	31.6g

* Percent Daily Values are based on a 2,000 calorie diet.

Creamy Coconut Cassava and Shrimp

Ingredients

- 1 lb yucca root, Peeled and chopped into 1inch pieces
- 2 tbsp olive oil
- 2 medium onions, chopped fine
- 4 ripe tomatoes, chopped fine
- 2 lbs small cooked peeled prawns
- 60 g coriander, chopped
- 100 g coconut cream, grated
- 1 1/2-3 tbsp palm oil
- 1 lime, quartered

Directions

- Bring a large salted pot of water to a boil. Cook in it the yucca root for 38 min. Drain it and mash it.
- Place a large pan over medium heat. Heat a splash of oil in it. Sauté in it the onion for 4 min.
- Stir in the tomato and cook them for 6 min. Add the prawns with coconut cream, a pinch of salt and pepper. Stir them until the cream melts.
- Stir in the coriander and mashed Yucca. Let them cook for 6 min. Stir in the palm oil. Serve your shrimp pan with some rice or noodles.
- Enjoy.

Servings Per Recipe: 4

Timing Information:

Preparation	15 mins
Total Time	35 mins

Nutritional Information:

Calories	589.2
Fat	18.9g
Cholesterol	285.7mg
Sodium	1324.2mg
Carbohydrates	70.8g
Protein	34.8g

* Percent Daily Values are based on a 2,000 calorie diet.

CHIPOTLE SHRIMPS

Ingredients

- 3 tsp olive oil
- 1 onion, finely chopped
- 6 tomatoes, peeled, diced
- 1/4 C. fresh flat-leaf parsley, finely chopped
- 1 lb shrimp, shelled, deveined, and cut into bite size pieces
- 1/2 tsp ground black pepper
- 1 tbsp butter
- 1 tbsp flour
- 1 (13 1/2 oz) cans coconut milk
- 1/2 tsp salt
- 1 small dried red pepper, minced
- 1 tsp dried chipotle powder

Directions

- Place a pot over medium heat. Heat a splash of oil in it. Sauté in it the onion for 3 min. Add the parsley with tomato and cook them for 6 min.
- Stir in the shrimp and cook them for 4 min. Add the melted butter with coconut milk, a pinch of salt and pepper then stir them well.
- Stir in the chipotle and cook them for an extra 4 min. Serve your stew warm with some rice.
- Enjoy.

Servings Per Recipe: 4

Timing Information:

| Preparation | 15 mins |
| Total Time | 30 mins |

Nutritional Information:

Calories	379.5
Fat	28.3g
Cholesterol	150.5mg
Sodium	993.9mg
Carbohydrates	15.7g
Protein	19.7g

* Percent Daily Values are based on a 2,000 calorie diet.

Pumpkin Bonbons

Ingredients

- 1 C. pumpkin puree
- 1 C. granulated sugar
- 2 C. grated coconut
- 1/4 tsp cinnamon
- 1/3 tsp ground cloves
- butter, for greasing
- confectioners' sugar, for dusting

Directions

- Place a large heavy saucepan over medium heat. Combine in it all the ingredients and cook them until they become slightly thick or reach 238 to 245 degrees F.
- Pour the mix in a greased baking dish to lose heat.
- Once the time is up, shape the mix into balls and coat them with some confectioner sugar. Serve them or store them in airtight containers.
- Enjoy.

Servings Per Recipe: 1

Timing Information:

Preparation	10 mins
Total Time	40 mins

Nutritional Information:

Calories	38.6
Fat	2.2g
Cholesterol	0.0mg
Sodium	1.3mg
Carbohydrates	4.9g
Protein	0.2g

* Percent Daily Values are based on a 2,000 calorie diet.

Thanks for Reading! Join the Club and Keep on Cooking with 6 More Cookbooks....

http://bit.ly/1TdrStv

To grab the box sets simply follow the link mentioned above, or tap one of book covers.

This will take you to a page where you can simply enter your email address and a PDF version of the box sets will be emailed to you.

Hope you are ready for some serious cooking!

http://bit.ly/1TdrStv

Come On...
Let's Be Friends :)

We adore our readers and love connecting with them socially.

Like BookSumo on Facebook and let's get social!

Facebook

And also check out the BookSumo Cooking Blog.

Food Lover Blog

Printed in Great Britain
by Amazon